# HIAWATHA'S BROTHERS

## A WILDLIFE RETROSPECTIVE

# HIAWATHA'S BROTHERS

## A WILDLIFE RETROSPECTIVE
### LOUIS J. VERME

AVANTI PUBLISHING
Munising, Michigan

Avanti Publishing
RR1 Box 598
Munising, MI 49862

Project coordination by Jenkins Group, Inc.

Book design by Group 5 Design

Cover painting by Frederic Remington

Printed in Hong Kong

1  3  5  7  9  10  8  6  4  2

Publisher's Cataloging-in-Publication Data
Verme, Louis, J.
Hiawatha's brothers : a wildlife
retrospective / Louis J. Verme. - Munising, Mich. : Avanti Pub., c1996
p.      col. ill.      cm.

Includes bibliographical references and index.

1. Natural history–Michigan–Upper Peninsula.
2. Mammals–Michigan–Upper Peninsula–History.
3. Big game and furbearers–Michigan–Upper Peninsula–History.
4. Upper Peninsula (Mich.)–History.
I. Title.
QH105.M5V47 1996
508.37'749 –dc20          95-77373

ISBN 0-9647282-0-6

For my Rose Marie

*some we loved*
*the loveliest and the best*

# CONTENTS

FOREWORD . . . . . . . . . . . . . . . . . . .11

PROLOGUE . . . . . . . . . . . . . . . . . . .13

Chapter 1  THE LAND BETWEEN THE LAKES . . . .17
    Physiography . . . . . . . . . . . . . . . .17
    Climate . . . . . . . . . . . . . . . . .18

Chapter 2  THE FOREST PRIMEVAL . . . . . . . . . .21
    Northern Hardwood Type . . . . . . . . . .21
    White Pine Type . . . . . . . . . . . . . .22
    White Cedar Type . . . . . . . . . . . . .24
    Overview . . . . . . . . . . . . . . . . .25

Chapter 3  THE INDIGENOUS YOOPERS . . . . . . .27
    The Ojibway People . . . . . . . . . . . .28
    Hunting Methods . . . . . . . . . . . . .32
    Use of Fire . . . . . . . . . . . . . . . .34
    The Savage Land . . . . . . . . . . . . .35
    Spiritual Codes . . . . . . . . . . . . . .37
    Trials and Tribulations . . . . . . . . . . .37
    Their Finest Hour . . . . . . . . . . . . .41

Chapter 4  THE FUR TRADE . . . . . . . . . . . . . . .43
    The *Coureurs Des Bois* . . . . . . . . . . . .43
    Michigan Fur Records (or Lack Thereof) . .49
    What Meant What . . . . . . . . . . . . . .51

Chapter 5  CLEARCUT AND BURN . . . . . . . . . . .55
    Charcoal and Pig Iron . . . . . . . . . . . .55
    "Daylight in the Swamp!" . . . . . . . . . .60
    When Pine was King . . . . . . . . . . . . .65
    Fire in the Forest . . . . . . . . . . . . .68
    From Past to Present . . . . . . . . . . . .73

Chapter 6  THE CERVIDS . . . . . . . . . . . . . . . .81
    White-tailed Deer . . . . . . . . . . . . . .81
    Moose . . . . . . . . . . . . . . . . . . .88
    Woodland Caribou . . . . . . . . . . . . . .90
    Elk . . . . . . . . . . . . . . . . . . . . .92

Chapter 7  WILD CANIDS . . . . . . . . . . . . . . . .95
    Wolf . . . . . . . . . . . . . . . . . . . .95
    Coyote . . . . . . . . . . . . . . . . . .101
    Red and Gray Fox . . . . . . . . . . . . .102

# CONTENTS

Chapter 8    CATS . . . . . . . . . . . . . . . . . . . . . . .103
             Mountain Lion . . . . . . . . . . . . . . . . . .103
             Lynx and Bobcat . . . . . . . . . . . . . . . .104


Chapter 9    WOLVERINES *ET AL.* . . . . . . . . . . . . .107
             Wolverine . . . . . . . . . . . . . . . . . . . . .107
             Marten and Fisher . . . . . . . . . . . . . . .108
             Otter and Badger . . . . . . . . . . . . . . . .110

Chapter 10    BEAVERS AND BEARS . . . . . . . . . . .113

EPILOGUE . . . . . . . . . . . . . . . . . . . . . . . . . . . .117
FOOTNOTES . . . . . . . . . . . . . . . . . . . . . . . . . .121
ACKNOWLEDGMENTS . . . . . . . . . . . . . . . . . . .125
BIBLIOGRAPHY . . . . . . . . . . . . . . . . . . . . . . .127
SCIENTIFIC NAMES . . . . . . . . . . . . . . . . . . . . .133
UPPER MICHIGAN MAMMALS . . . . . . . . . . . . . .135
GLOSSARY . . . . . . . . . . . . . . . . . . . . . . . . . . .137
A NOTE ON HIAWATHA . . . . . . . . . . . . . . . . . .139
INDEX . . . . . . . . . . . . . . . . . . . . . . . . . . . . . .141
ORDER INFORMATION . . . . . . . . . . . . . . . . . .143

# LIST OF ILLUSTRATIONS

Geologic zones in Michigan . . . . . . . . . . . . . . . . . .16

Snowfall contour map for Upper Michigan . . . . . . . .19

Northern hardwoods great blue heronry . . . . . . . . . .20

Estivant pine grove near Copper Harbor . . . . . . . . . .22

Hartwick Pines State Park near Grayling . . . . . . . . .23

Hunting method used by early Indians . . . . . . . . . . .27

Ecologic/food resources in Great Lakes region . . . . .28

Bas-relief of Hiawatha and "brothers"
in Munising post office . . . . . . . . . . . . . . . . . . . . . .30

Indian and the lily painting by
George de Forest Brush . . . . . . . . . . . . . . . . . . . . . .31

Samuel de Champlain's sketch of Indian
deer drive in southeastern Ontario . . . . . . . . . . . . . .33

Statue of Father Marquette in his namesake city . . . .38

Jesuit Fathers' map of Upper Michigan . . . . . . . . . .39

Chapel Rock beach near Munising . . . . . . . . . . . . . .40

Iroquois Point lighthouse near Sault Ste. Marie . . . . .41

Painting of Radisson and Grosseilliers by
Frederic Remington . . . . . . . . . . . . . . . . . . . . . . . . .42

Historic beaver distribution in North America . . . . . .44

French-Canadian voyageurs and
birch bark cargo canoes . . . . . . . . . . . . . . . . . . . . . .45

French River travel route of
voyageurs to Lake Huron . . . . . . . . . . . . . . . . . . . .46

Present-day view of Sault Ste. Marie rapids . . . . . . .46

Reconstructed Fort Michilimackinac . . . . . . . . . . . .47

Fur trading routes centered at Fort Michilimackinac . .48

Historic Grand Portage on Lake Superior
near Pigeon River . . . . . . . . . . . . . . . . . . . . . . . . . .49

Route of the voyageurs from Montreal to
Great Slave Lake . . . . . . . . . . . . . . . . . . . . . . . . . . .50

American Fur Company cabin originally
on Grand Island . . . . . . . . . . . . . . . . . . . . . . . . . . .52

Canvas-covered recreational canoe . . . . . . . . . . . . . .53

Location of Upper Michigan blast furnaces . . . . . . . .54

Schoolcraft Iron Co. furnace near Munising . . . . . . .56

Ruins of Onota (Bay Furnace) site . . . . . . . . . . . . . .57

Remnant charcoal kilns near Marquette . . . . . . . . . .57

Historic townsite buildings at Fayette State Park . . . .58

Homestead log cabin of
Charles Paulson in Alger County . . . . . . . . . . . . . . .59

Early railroad grades used in
logging the Cusino Swamp . . . . . . . . . . . . . . . . . . .61

Ancient "horse barn" near Cusino Swamp . . . . . . . . .62

ILLUSTRATIONS

Location of major railroad lines in
Upper Michigan ca. 1910 . . . . . . . . . . . . . . . . . . .63

Pristine distribution of pine stands in Upper Michigan. 64

Trainload of white pine logs near Newberry . . . . . . .66

Lumbermens' Monument near Oscoda
in Lower Michigan . . . . . . . . . . . . . . . . . . . . . . .67

Paul Bunyan and Babe, his blue ox . . . . . . . . . . . . .68

Stark vista of Kingston Plains pine barrens . . . . . . .69

Remnant pine at Evelyn Plains near Shingleton . . . .69

Sharp-tailed grouse on pine plains dancing ground . . .70

Railroad grades in early hardwood slashings . . . . . .71

Abandoned Petrel Grade railway . . . . . . . . . . . . . . .71

Abandoned farm in Menominee County . . . . . . . . . .72

Abortive attempt to farm marshland
via drainage ditches . . . . . . . . . . . . . . . . . . . . . . .73

Reintroduced trumpeter swans at
Seney National Wildlife Refuge . . . . . . . . . . . . . . .74

Autumn vista of paper birch-rimmed lake . . . . . . . .75

Fireweed on burned-over site . . . . . . . . . . . . . . . . .76

Michigan DNR prescribed burn in
clearcut cedar swamp . . . . . . . . . . . . . . . . . . . . . .77

Natural revegetation on cedar clearcut burn . . . . . . .78

Sketch by Ozz Warbach on importance of aspen . . . . .79

The lure of the deer hunting season . . . . . . . . . . . . .80

Correlation of sapling cedar acreage
and buck hunting success . . . . . . . . . . . . . . . . . . . .82

Temporal relationships between browse production
and shelter provision of cedar swamps . . . . . . . . . . .83

Skulking deer in conifer yard in midwinter . . . . . . . .84

Moose airlift during recent restocking effort . . . . . . .89

Extirpation of Michigan mammals . . . . . . . . . . . . . .91

Captive wolf "Queenie" at
Cusino Wildlife Research Station . . . . . . . . . . . . . . .99

Portrait of a lynx . . . . . . . . . . . . . . . . . . . . . . . . .104

Portrait of a bobcat . . . . . . . . . . . . . . . . . . . . . . .105

Extant taxidermy mount of a Michigan wolverine . . .106

Reintroducing the marten to Michigan . . . . . . . . . .108

A porcupine at bay . . . . . . . . . . . . . . . . . . . . . . . .109

The playful otter is a skilled fisherman . . . . . . . . . .111

Giant-sized beaver lodge . . . . . . . . . . . . . . . . . . . .114

"Blanket" beaver pelts once were extremely valuable . .114

Sow black bear and cubs at den site . . . . . . . . . . . .115

Scene from *Bedtime Stories* by Thornton W. Burgess . .117

Drumming-pose of "Charlie," a tame ruffed grouse . .118

The staunch pose of "Bandit" locked on point . . . . . .120

# FOREWORD

The Upper Peninsula of Michigan is unique. Its geology, geography, flora, fauna and people combine to provide an ambiance found nowhere else. Travelers crossing the Straits of Mackinac feel they have entered a forest primeval. It isn't quite that now, of course, but instead consists of a region tempered and aged by people, yielding a landscape mosaic inhabited by a wide variety of vegetation and wildlife. This mix of habitats, from deep cedar swamps to upland, arid, sandy plains, lakes and rivers adjacent to our largest, deepest, clearest and coldest Great Lake, is difficult to interpret and appreciate just by driving along highways US-2 and M-28.

This book gives the reader an in-depth understanding of how various physical, biological and human factors have impinged on the original situation to produce the current landscape or biome.

What better person to act as this interpreter than Louis J. Verme, who has spent more than four decades "in the woods" trying to decipher the ecological nature of this complex environment. Lou has emphasized the study of white-tailed deer, but this involved gaining a sound knowledge of the many habitat types occupied by deer, and the combination of plant and animal species associated with deer. He has an outstanding record of technical publications on many phases of deer biology and ecology. But this book, written without the scientific jargon required by science editors, provides the reader with enjoyable essays that increase one's appreciation of the Upper Peninsula.

Tramping through the cedar bogs on snowshoes at 30 below, and sweating and swatting blackflies during spring fawn searches, allows for periods of reflection on how this all came about. In his retirement, Lou has had the opportunity to integrate his long years of field experience and thus synthesize some ideas that more adequately form a cohesive historical perspective as to what was important in influencing the changes in Upper Michigan's landscape, hence the often drastic fluctuations in its wildlife populations. The human impact on the forest primeval began hundreds of years ago, and people are still having a great impact on the environment, thereby greatly modifying the fauna and flora. Lou has provided a sociological as well as a natural history of the Upper Peninsula in order to give readers a clear insight, not only about what happened here and when, but most importantly how all the pieces of the ecological puzzle fit together to form the true picture.

His book can be highly recommended to those who are considering a first trip to the U. P., those who have traveled widely, and even (perhaps especially) those who have lived in this land their entire lives. A careful reading will enrich our knowledge and appreciation of this most interesting region, either while passing through or diligently exploring it.

**Tony J. Peterle**
Ohio State University
Columbus, Ohio

# PROLOGUE

*There are some who can live without wild things, and some who cannot. These essays are the delights and dilemmas of one who cannot.*

**–Aldo Leopold**
*A Sand County Almanac*

For nearly 35 years the author was employed by the Department of Natural Resources as a biologist at the Cusino Wildlife Research Station, Shingleton, in Michigan's Upper Peninsula. Long before reaching one's usual retirement age I pondered, with some trepidation, how I would spend my unfettered days once that fateful time arrived. Various colleagues urged me to write a definitive treatise on the white-tailed deer, my research specialty. Alas, the Wildlife Management Institute beat me to the punch by publishing in 1984 a tome on the ecology and management of this magnificent beast, for which I co-authored a chapter on its physiology and nutrition. Hence it was necessary to pursue another challenging cerebral endeavor to help me retain some semblance of sanity in the life ahead.

Over the years I became increasingly aware that a comprehensive critical analysis did not exist documenting the tremendous population fluctuations that occurred among game animals and furbearers native to Upper Michigan following exploration and exploitation of the land by Europeans. This lack of information is understandable because relevant historical lore is scanty at best, often inaccurate, and at worst quite misleading. Prior to the 1800s, for example, records on the subject consisted of anecdotal accounts representing the opinions of untrained observers who were more interested in describing human activities and places visited than in authoring a scientific dissertation on the fauna and flora encountered in their travels. Even reports in the early 1900s are open to question regarding the validity of data presented (if any), and it requires considerable detective-work and interpretation based on professional knowledge and insight to separate fact from fiction as to the probable abundance of a particular species for a specific era.

Given these notable shortcomings I decided to write an historical retrospective dealing with some wildlife common to Michigan's Upper Peninsula, a unique region having a long and colorful past. Parochially the area is known as the U.P., and its citizens affectionately referred to as "Yoopers," for more or less obvious reasons. This work began as a labor of love, but soon became an obsession. Considering my background I thought the project would be a "piece-of-cake;" however, subsequent events showed there was no basis for such naive expectations. The outcome will not please everybody; scholars may find my essay wanting in substance if not in style, whereas cursory readers might conclude that it tells them more about "kangaroos" than they really care to know about such critters. The text is intended primarily for knowledgeable students who want to learn more precisely how temporal ecological events influenced the welfare and thus the population dynamics of our more important animals, especially the larger mammals. Hopefully this synthesis will not only enlighten but also stimulate inquisitive readers to undertake their own research on the topics treated in this book.

**Louis J. Verme**
Munising, Michigan

# HIAWATHA'S BROTHERS

## A WILDLIFE RETROSPECTIVE

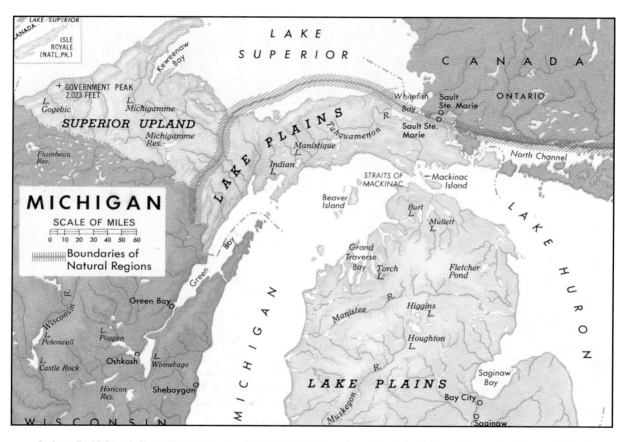

*Geologically, Michigan's Upper Peninsula can be divided into two halves, the eastern Lake Plains and the western Superior Upland. The uplands are among the oldest rocks on Earth, possibly 4.5 billion years old, formed by igneous magma. In sharp contrast, the Lake Plains, covering the east half of the U.P. and the entire Lower Peninsula, are mainly of sedimentary origin, consisting of sandstone/limestone strata deposited over hundreds of millions of years. Many of the smaller glacial lakes have filled in with plant debris, creating muck and peat bogs. (F.E. Compton & Co.)*

# 1

# _ THE LAND BETWEEN THE LAKES _

## PHYSIOGRAPHY

Geologically, Michigan's Upper Peninsula can be divided roughly in two by a line meandering from Marquette southward to Iron Mountain, thence almost to Menominee. The western portion, or Superior Uplands, consists of rugged hills and rock outcrops of igneous (some metamorphic) origin formed several billion years ago during the Precambrian era. This mineral-rich landmass (copper-iron-gold) constitutes the southern edge of the Canadian, or Laurentian, Shield. In sharp contrast, the eastern half of the U.P., the Lake Plains, is relatively flat and comprised of numerous layers of sedimentary rock (sandstone-lime-stone-dolomite-shale) deposited during the Paleozoic era 200 - 500 million years ago. Glaciation during the Pleistocene era (beginning over two million years ago) occurred in four distinct stages with warm intervals in between, which melted the icecap and periodically inundated the region. Northward retreat of the last, or Wisconsin, glacier 10,000 - 14,000 years ago poured great quantities of water into the Great Lakes basin through rapid melting, while rebound of the land after glacier melt altered former outlets, flooding the land to its highest level, and forming Lake Nipissing 3,500 - 4,500 years ago. This watershed decreased in size to present-day Lake Superior around 2,500 years ago. Upper Michigan now consists of roughly 10 million acres, equal to 16 thousand square miles.

The slowly retreating icemass left behind vast deposits of sand as outwash plains, and an assortment of glacial till ranging from colloidal clay to granite boulders, often in a heterogeneous mixture. Gravelly terminal moraines, drumlins, and other landforms were created as the ice melted or pushed forward. Glacial melt gave rise to myriad small lakes and potholes. Some of these slowly filled in with woody or herbaceous remains, ultimately producing a variety of organic soils ranging from highly acid, poorly decomposed woody peats to finely-textured granular mucks of slightly alkaline or neutral pH situated over limestone or dolomite. Upland soils vary from thin accumulations over bedrock, relatively deep clay beds, to those consisting of silt and loams or coarse sand and gravel. Some mineral soils on level ground become seasonally waterlogged, while others on steep knolls are excessively dry in summer. The cool, moist climate results in severe leaching of organic matter and minerals from the upper soil horizons, forming the gray or gray-brown podzols typical of mesic temperate forests. Thick sub-surface mineralized hard-pans are common in many soils as a result.

# CLIMATE

The U.P. "enjoys" a maritime climate owing to the ameliorative influence of Lake Superior to the north and Lakes Michigan and Huron on the south shore and eastern tip, respectively. Comparative statistics for Superior alone are impressive: a maximum length of 350 miles, 160 miles wide, a surface area of nearly 32,000 square miles, up to 1,330 feet deep, yielding a volume of 2,860 cubic miles. The water of all three lakes warms slowly in spring and, conversely, retains its heat until midautumn. Hence spring arrives late, but Indian summer lingers well into October as a result of the great amount of thermal energy stored in these immense bathtubs. Summers are short and cool; despite the moderating influence of Lake Superior in particular, killing frosts occur even in July. It would be difficult to convince an avid gardener in, say, Shingleton, that global warming due to the so-called greenhouse effect is in fact a reality. (Suffice to say that the 1992 summer was the coldest in memory, caused by the eruption of Philippine volcano Mount Pinatubo the year before!)

U.P. winters are notoriously harsh and protracted. Unlike in Camelot, there is no legal limit to the snow here, and winter is not forbidden till December; thus when winter comes, spring can indeed be far behind. Based on amount of snowfall, the region can be bisected latitudinally by a line roughly following highway M-28. Prevailing northerly winds sweeping across Lake Superior pick up moisture from the warmer water and promptly dump it as "snow-showers" along the shoreline as the air cools while crossing the colder mainland. These sometimes constant lake-effect flurries can soon accumulate to knee depth during early winter. Total snowfall in this sector commonly exceeds 200 - 250 inches, resulting in a snowpack 3-4 feet deep by midwinter. The Lake Michigan watershed, a few miles southward, receives much less snow, however, and consequently is facetiously referred to as the "banana-belt" by the more masochistic (and envious) residents to the north. Except for periodic and frequently severe blizzards, snowfall tends to diminish as the Great Lakes gradually freeze. Lake Superior froze over completely during the seemingly interminably bitter cold 1993-94 winter, as it also did in 1978-79. Predictably, minimum temperatures become progressively lower as extensive ice forms.

Whereas stable low temperatures north of Lake Superior (i.e. in Ontario) help keep the more limited snowfall there in a powdery form, occasional drizzle and sleet storms or unseasonable thaws markedly influence the snowpack's composition southward. Here the formation of several crust layers of varying thickness and hardness controls the snow's supportive quality. This characteristic is of crucial importance to a host of wild animals, especially cervids. Winter temperatures commonly remain below freezing, often sub-zero, for weeks or months. The resultant air chill, horrendous on a calm, clear night because of radiant energy exchange to the cold sky, is greatly exacerbated through thermal convection by gale winds or a blizzard. If adequate overhead cover to minimize body heat loss is not readily available, or existing food supplies cannot replenish sapped energy, winter often proves fatal to many animals through acute malnutrition and exposure.

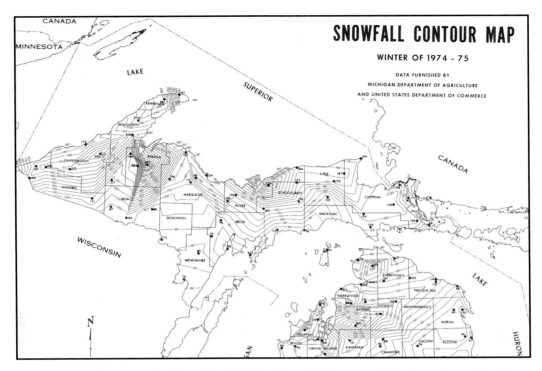

*Upper Michigan's climate is greatly influenced by Lakes Superior and Michigan in particular. Seasonal snowfall varies considerably from north to south, roughly following highway M-28, which bisects the region. Cities like Calumet and Munising receive some of the heaviest snowfall in the continental U.S. (excluding mountain elevations), mostly dumped in December and January because of the Lake Superior "effect" on prevailing weather. (Michigan Department Agriculture and U.S. Department Commerce.)*

Approximately one-half of the 30 - 35 inches of annual precipitation falls as rain during the growing season for woody plants. The high soil moisture and humid ambient provide good growing conditions for the environmentally-adapted trees despite the short summers. Severe droughts are rare, but long dry spells commonly prevail. Although not located in tornado-alley per se, the U.P. is sporadically subject to violent windstorms at any season, sometimes causing extensive limb breakage or uprooting of trees. The considerable water surface in and around the peninsula encourages cloud formation, hence sunny days are rather limited or of short duration. Strong air masses, or fronts, continually sweep through the peninsula or collide here, giving meaning to a local adage — if you don't like the weather, just wait a minute!

*Most of Upper Michigan originally was covered by northern hardwoods, the climax type on the richer soils. Although these forests are not attractive to most larger animals, great blue herons like to nest in the crowns of tall trees. Probably for reasons of security, such rookeries often support several dozen mated pairs of birds. Logging of these unique sites would constitute desecration. Visits by bird-watchers are to be discouraged to prevent site abandonment or increased risk of predation on fledglings.*

# 2

# THE FOREST PRIMEVAL

**M**ichigan's Upper Peninsula lies in an ecological tension zone representing the transitional stage between the boreal forest *(taiga)* north of Lake Superior and the northern hardwood type to the south. The maritime climate "holds back" the arctic influence which favors the spruce-fir biome northward. Our forest cover is complex because the soil types are so complex, thanks to the mixing effect of the various glaciers.

## NORTHERN HARDWOOD TYPE

The settlers found most of this region covered by hardwood forests comprised predominantly of sugar maple, beech, yellow birch, basswood, and elm, species which grow best on productive soils — clay, fine sandy loams, etc. Hemlock becomes an important component in many stands, especially those on wetter sites or moist north-facing slopes. Yellow birch is not as tolerant of shade as are its associates, and probably reproduced itself in virgin stands only after some disturbance exposed mineral soil, which is to its liking. Hemlock likewise requires fresh earth or rotting wood for successful seedling survival. Lack of hemlock reproduction, even below snowline, in many instances has been conveniently blamed on deer winter browsing damage, whereas the more likely culprit was unsuitable growing conditions. Sugar maple is a highly competitive, ubiquitous species. On the lighter sandy loams and more pervious heavier soils, sugar maple is unusually aggressive in perpetuating itself. On drier, hillier slopes it may dominate the stand to the virtual exclusion of associate species. Given good soil fertility and ample moisture, sugar maples in forest stands commonly grow 80-100 feet tall and 2-3 feet in diameter; old-growth trees on Grand Island once reached this spectacular size, for example. Beech, a late arrival from the east, thrives best on calcium-rich (limestone) sites scattered within the east-half of the U.P., whereas basswood dominates on the richest soils of the acidic Canadian Shield. (Beech is an excellent tree for wildlife because its starchy nutlets are so nourishing; unfortunately, large mast crops are produced only at irregular intervals.)

The classical concept of a climax forest, a static plant community that maintains itself in place *ad infinitum*, is today undergoing revision. New evidence, based mainly on results of pollen analysis for peat bogs, now suggests that forest composition in the Upper Great Lakes has slowly changed as new species arrived in response to glacial retreat, and cycles of colder, then warmer, and again colder weather over past millennia. Although the boreal forest occupied large acreage in this region a few thousand years ago, only remnants of this forest type are found here now. The spruce-fir understory almost always disappears after the hardwood canopy is removed (logged) and the site warms up and becomes drier. Presently beech drops out of the forest barely north of Sault Ste. Marie, while sugar maple and yellow birch vanish about 50 and 100 miles farther north, respectively. Some scientists investigating global warming predict that rising temperature within the next century will effect a shift in range of hundreds of miles northward for these species, to a point above the discontinuous permafrost line of today. By the same token one would expect the central deciduous forest to encroach northward to replace the hardwood species currently here. The prospect of having oak-hickory woods in the U.P. in the foreseeable future is mind-boggling! But this forecast may simply be a worst-case scenario, since there is still much debate among scientists about the exact nature and extent of global warming. Moreover, shifts in geographic distribution of forest types probably require a longer time than assumed. (One authority even postulates that Kirtland's warbler, which nests only in a small area in northern Lower Michigan, could lose its entire breeding habitat within 30 years if projected climatic change eliminates the jack pine stands currently growing on these sandy sites. But this seems to be a highly questionable timetable in my opinion.)

*Ecologically distinct from the cathedral-like Hartwick Pines downstate, the Estivant Pines near Copper Harbor are impressive in their own right. This stand consists of ancient trees scattered among northern hardwoods growing on productive soil. A notable lack of white pine reproduction indicates that this species will not replace itself after these veterans topple at overmaturity, unless a natural disaster again prepares a favorable seedbed.*

# WHITE PINE TYPE

The legendary white pine forests actually occupied only 10-15 percent of the U.P.'s landmass, or roughly 1.0-1.5 million acres. White pine was present in virtually all stands as individual trees, often growing on the best sites to the gigantic size of 150 or more feet tall and exceeding 5 feet in diameter for the butt log. Such specimens were known as "cork" pine because the extra thick bark allowed them to float high on river drives. Being less shade-tolerant than the surrounding northern hardwoods, the fast-growing pines may have became established in upland stands on the newly-exposed mounds of mineral soil around the

*The majestic Hartwick Pines eventually will blow down but may rise again from the ashes of an accompanying lightning fire,
thus repeating the cycle of stand regeneration periodically experienced over millennia since the last glacier. This remnant stand of tall trees
inspires awe among multitudes of visitors annually.*

roots of windthrown trees, and soon overtopped the innately shorter hardwoods. However, ecologist Forest Stearns believes that these pines represented individuals that had survived earlier massive blowdown and/or fire, and that hardwoods filled in beneath these remnant trees. A noted U.P. scientist remarked that while on a forestry field trip in the early 1940s the students walked through the vaunted D'Estivant Pines [sic] in the Keweenaw Peninsula without recognizing them because their expectations of this pristine stand greatly exceeded reality as to their size and abundance.

Clearly, however, the bulk of the white pine occurred as huge groves (some of them tens of thousands of acres in extent), often admixed with various other species, typically growing in scattered pockets of sandy outwash plains.[1] These pines, generally comprising even-aged stands, grew to moderate size, mainly 20-30 inches in diameter, depending upon inherent soil fertility. Yet the board-foot volume contained in virgin stands was often enormous. In some instances the trees were so large, hence widely spaced, that one could drive a wagon through the area without entanglement because heavy shade had eliminated the underbrush.

Ecologists still disagree as to how white pine forests originated. There are silvical reasons to believe that the 400-year "Little Ice Age," a period of highly unsettled climate with great extremes in precipitation and temperature that began in the late 1400s, stimulated an increase in white pine (as well as hemlock). Oddly enough, this period followed on the heels of the balmy Medieval Warm Epoch, peaking perhaps 1,000 years ago, which enabled the Vikings to explore westward to Greenland and beyond. Although white pine is better adapted than are the northern hard-

woods to withstand cold, the question arises as to what grew on these relatively poor sites if not the pines. Some stands, most notably the remnant Hartwick Pines in northern Lower Michigan, are believed to have developed in the path of a tornado or windstorm that devastated an older such forest. Another scientist hypothesized that intense sunspot activity 400 - 500 years ago led to widespread drought, and that resultant wildfires were responsible for generating the pine type. Fire favors white pine regeneration because its seed can germinate even in fresh ash, as do those of jack pine — the "fire-climax" species. (Red pine has more exacting seedbed requirments, and does not germinate well in soil with high concentrations of ash.) The most convincing evidence supports the viewpoint that wildfires, sometimes following blowdowns, repeatedly occurred at about the end of white pine's normal lifespan of 250 - 300 years. According to a noted Midwest ecologist, "In some places, at least 25 generations of pine had occurred over a period of 6,000 to 8,000 years" from seed supplied by neighboring unburned trees, which produce bumper cone crops at 3- to 10-year intervals.

# WHITE CEDAR TYPE

The white cedar type constitutes about two million acres of commercial forest land in the Upper Great Lakes, roughly one-half of which is found in the U.P., mainly in the vast swampland of the eastern sector. White cedar is considered only moderately shade tolerant, which poses the question of how it reproduced itself in fairly pure stands when species that thrive in shade also like wet environments. White cedar is exceptionally long-lived, however, often exceeding 400 years in age, hence far longer than competing associates. Silviculturist Carl Tubbs reasoned that as these overmature stands began to break down, considerable dead wood accumulated on the forest floor. Then it was only a matter of time before a lightning strike on a tall snag ignited the dry fuel. The resultant conflagration consumed all but the larger branches, and reduced the ground debris to ash, thereby providing a favorable growing medium for windblown cedar seed.

Empirical evidence indicates that many if not most even-aged white cedar stands existing today originated after fire swept through the area following logging. A study which colleague William Johnston and I conducted left little doubt that broadcast burning of clearcut swamps benefits white cedar regeneration by eliminating the thick slash that would otherwise impede seed germination. Moreover, fire kills the advanced stems of competing hardwoods or other conifers that frequently dominate cut-over sites for years, and burning recycles the nutrients (nitrogen, potassium, and phosphorus) bound up in the litter which otherwise only slowly decomposes. Since soil moisture remains fairly high near the surface from capillary action, only the top few inches of organic debris are consumed despite a hot fire. The sum effect of swamp fires decisively favors perpetuation of even-aged white cedar. In nature, swamps probably burned in patches, yielding a mosaic of stands, each differing in age by several decades or more. However, on some wet sites (except peatlands), cedar often occurred in an admixture of tree species that tolerate seasonally water-logged roots. Although cedar is commonly found in somewhat acidic swamps, it grows best on organic soils of neutral or basic pH; it also thrives on limestone outcrops in uplands.

# OVERVIEW

It should by now be apparent that the pristine U.P. was not a relatively uniform "deep-dark-forest" of murmuring pines and hemlocks, but instead consisted of a heterogeneous assemblage of tree groups varying widely in age, species composition, structure, and density. Natural catastrophes were the rule, not the exception. Research in the Boundary Waters Canoe Area of Minnesota, for instance, revealed that major fires had burned many portions of this wilderness area about every quarter-century over the past several hundred years. Possibly the entire tract was burned over at least every century. Once a fire got started in old-growth conifer forests, nothing but a heavy rainstorm could put it out, especially if it "crowned." Additionally, sporadic tornados, ice storms, severe insect infestations, fungal outbreaks, and floodings continually modified the primeval forests, thus contributing to its diverse pattern. Many such events were not trifling matters but covered hundreds of square miles, as still periodically occurs even today under far different environmental conditions. For example, a furious summer windstorm in northern Wisconsin in 1977 flattened a swath of timber 166 miles long and 17 miles wide (40,000 acres), the result of several dozen violent downdrafts. Natural anomalies like marshes (fens) and bogs, lakes and streams, and beaver meadows also contributed to canopy fragmentation and habitat edge sought after by various animals. Frequent site disturbance helped maintain a rich diversity of plant life favored by certain wildlife. Many of these ecologic episodes were ephemeral, however, and wildlife species continually "shopped-around" to find their favorite niche.

# 3

# THE INDIGENOUS YOOPERS

*By the shores of Gitche Gumee,*
*By the shining Big-Sea-Water,*
*Stood the wigwam of Nokomis,*
*Daughter of the Moon, Nokomis.*
*Dark behind it rose the forest,*
*Rose the black and gloomy pine-trees,*
*Rose the firs with cones upon them;*
*Bright before it beat the water,*
*Beat the clear and sunny water,*
*Beat the shining Big-Sea-Water.*

*There the wrinkled old Nokomis*
*Nursed the little Hiawatha....*

*During the Early Archaic Period (ca. 9,000-6,000 B.C.), Asian "immigrants" to Michigan hunted moose and caribou with crude spears, often used with a thrower, or atlatl, to give it greater velocity, hence deeper penetration, on thick-skinned beasts. The men had immense strength and stamina, reputedly being able to run down even white-tailed deer after a fresh snow in relays, or, as shown here, on snowshoes when moose floundered in deep or crusted snow and soon became exhausted. Every bit of the carcass was utilized for food, clothing, or implements. (Michigan State University Museum.)*

So wrote Henry Wadsworth Longfellow in his epic poem The Song of Hiawatha. Longfellow acknowledged that this saga was based upon an anthology of Indian myths and legends published earlier by Henry Rowe Schoolcraft, who had served as U.S. Indian Agent at Sault Ste. Marie and Mackinac Island from 1822 to 1836. Longfellow also mentioned that "the scene of the poem is among the Ojibways on the southern shore of Lake Superior, in the region between the Pictured Rocks and the Grand Sable." This, of course, is the present-day locale of the Pictured Rocks National Lakeshore which stretches from Munising eastward along many miles of high sandstone cliffs, sprawling beaches, and windswept dunes to Grand Marais. (I know this fascinating area well, having worked and played here for two-score years.)

# THE OJIBWAY PEOPLE

Aboriginal immigrants to the U.P.,(perhaps as early as 11,000 B.C.) who lived here from A.D. 400 to A.D. 1630 are referred to by anthropologists as the Late Woodland Indians. They survived by hunting, fishing, and gathering wild fruits and seeds. The earlier cultures, at least, were semi-nomadic and not exceedingly warlike. The tribes in the boreal forest north and west of Lake Superior subsisted primarily through hunting of big game (moose and caribou) and smaller mammals (beaver and hare), and by fishing. West of Lake Michigan and south of Lake Superior, in northern Wisconsin and eastern Minnesota, the more limey shallow flowages and marshes favored the growth of wild rice, which permitted a life-style based substantially on this grain, augmented by fish and game. In parts of Michigan

and Wisconsin where rudimentary agriculture was climatically feasible, cultivated crops, notably corn (maize), squash, and beans, were important food items. Like wild rice, corn and beans were stored dry in large quantities until needed in emergencies. However, such gardening was limited to areas with at least 120 frost-free days for beans and squash, whereas 140 days were necessary to ripen corn (consequently, because of early frosts, the ears

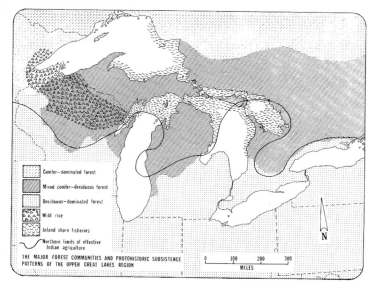

Comfer—dominated forest
Mixed conifer—deciduous forest
Deciduous—dominated forest
Wild rice
Inland shore fisheries
Northern limits of effective Indian agriculture

THE MAJOR FOREST COMMUNITIES AND PROTOHISTORIC SUBSISTENCE PATTERNS OF THE UPPER GREAT LAKES REGION

0    100    200    300
MILES

N

*Indians of the Upper Great Lakes were hunter/gatherers, tenaciously making do with whatever bounty nature provided. Wild rice constituted a staple food in Wisconsin and Minnesota, but the plants did not grow well in the more acidic waters of Upper Michigan. The short, cool summers here made cultivation of basic agricultural crops like corn and beans an unreliable venture because they often did not ripen before a hard frost hit in late summer. (University Minnesota Press.)*

commonly had to be eaten while still green, or fire-dried). Advent of the Little Ice Age therefore forced tribes living in the Great Lakes region to revert to being hunter/gatherers for their existence.

Although venison and other meat could be kept frozen or dried/smoked for later use, such game was obtained in quantity only during certain seasons. Fish could also be preserved in this manner, but unlike mammals, they were caught year round from open water or through the ice if need be. The Ojibway were highly skilled fishermen, being adept at making and using gill nets, seines, spears, as well as crude bone hooks and lures to catch their staple food supply. Great numbers of whitefish, lake trout, and sturgeon were taken at and below the St. Marys River rapids, especially when schooled for spawning. Entire villages, even far-away tribes, made extensive trips to Sault Ste. Marie in summer, returning on foot or by canoe before freeze-up. Another traditional trek was from Little Bay de Noc(ette) to Munising, an overland journey across the peninsula of 35 - 40 miles. Why these people made this seasonal trip remains an enigma to me, since surely the stocks of fish were no greater in Munising Bay and environs. Both areas presumably had similar blueberry crops, and the blackflies and mosquitos no doubt were as plentiful near Grand Island as at Bay de Noc. Perhaps the summer encampment was primarily a social event which allowed people to maintain close friendships and family ties with distant clans or tribes. A Jesuit missionary noted that the Indians near Lake Nipissing gathered together to fish and cultivate crops "more for pleasure and that they may have fresh food to eat, than for their [own] support."

The Ojibway also made maple syrup and sugar in spring, which provided a critical energy source after a hard winter. This sugaring likewise comprised a useful communal activity before the rivers and coast became ice-free for travel in late spring. Like other Indians, the Ojibway were a product of centuries of cultural adaptation to a specific way of life dictated by their surroundings. That is, they were so accustomed to living in the sugar maple-dominated forest that in the Seventeenth Century they migrated from Sault Ste. Marie along the north shore of Lake Superior only as far as Michipicoten Bay, where the boreal forest reaches the coast. "They could travel no farther and keep company with the maple," as one historian succinctly put it. The Indians were consummate naturalists — they had to be to eke out a hardscrabble existence in this harsh, unforgiving land. To leave an ecological setting they knew so well, notably the medicinal and sustenance value of every plant, plus the haunts and habits of fish and game, and start over in an unfamiliar setting was simply unthinkable.

The men were superb hunters; their uncanny ability to stalk noiselessly through the forest unquestionably was true. This lore was passed on from father to son over the ages, as it was vital to the welfare of a family group. Such learning probably was a personal challenge (and surely also fun) for youngsters, as Longfellow depicted for Hiawatha:

> *Of all beasts he learned the language,*
> *Learned their names and all their secrets,*
> *How the beavers built their lodges,*
> *Where the squirrels hid their acorns,*
> *How the reindeer ran so swiftly,*
> *Why the rabbit was so timid,*
> *Talked with them whene'er he met them,*
> *Called them 'Hiawatha's Brothers'.*

Although the pioneers were rightfully awed by the Indians' ability to kill game with bow and arrow, this activity required more time and energy than most hunters could easily afford, and the method yielded relatively modest

*A whimsical bas-relief depicting Hiawatha and his figurative "brothers" adorns a wall of the Munising Post Office, by the shores of Gitche Gumee. Sculptor Hugo Robus caught the nuance of Longfellow's epic tale wherein the Ojibway youth became a close friend to local mammals so as to "learn all their secrets." The mural was done under the auspices of the WPA when the building was erected in 1937, and has become an historic artifact, conceivably a national treasure.*

*The Indian was at home in the wilderness, which, conversely, terrified most whites. Of necessity they became highly skilled hunters, knowing the ways of all game animals. The brave in this scene, painted by George de Forest Brush, could pass as the fabled Hiawatha, seeking the famous red deer, which he killed with a single arrow "by the ford across the river." (Berry-Hill Galleries.)*

returns. Bow hunting was reserved mainly for ritualistic purposes, or times when food was urgently needed for the hunter's well-being or to save his kin. Longfellow caught the mood of the quest, wherein Iagoo, the story-teller and friend of old Nokomis, made a bow for the youth:

> Then he said to Hiawatha:
> 'Go, my son, into the forest,
> Where the red deer herd together,
> Kill for us a famous roebuck,
> Kill for us a deer with antlers!'

> Forth into the forest straightway
> All alone walked Hiawatha
> Proudly, with his bow and arrows;

Later, as the elusive quarry walked down the woodland pathway, he saw his chance:

> Then, upon one knee uprising,
> Hiawatha aimed an arrow;
> Scarce a twig moved with his motion,
> Scarce a leaf was stirred or rustled,
> But the wary roebuck started,
> Stamped with all his hoofs together,
> Listened with one foot uplifted,
> Leaped as if to meet the arrow;
> Ah! the singing, fatal arrow,
> Like a wasp it buzzed and stung him!

> Dead he lay there in the forest,
> By the ford across the river;
> Beat his timid heart no longer,

> But the heart of Hiawatha
> Throbbed and shouted and exaulted,
> As he bore the red deer homeward,
> And Iagoo and Nokomis
> Hailed his coming with applauses.

Any novice bowhunter can empathize with Hiawatha's understandable euphoria at killing his first whitetail buck, the wariest animal of all big game.

# HUNTING METHODS

As a rule, communal hunting, which resulted in a large number of kills on a single venture, far outweighed lone hunting (stalking) in terms of its importance to tribal subsistence. Among northern Indians, many if not most white-tailed deer were taken by group hunting when the animals were congregated and in prime condition, as during the rut or early winter. However, deer and other cervids were taken opportunistically in all seasons by individual hunters if the occasion arose — as any smart predator would do. Indians were adept at using every means imaginable to efficiently kill game, including deadfalls, pitfalls, snares, baiting and lures, even the use of dogs.

In 1615, French explorer Samuel de Champlain observed a band of Huron Indians in the vicinity of Georgian Bay, Ontario, employ a deer drive to slaughter these animals:

> "... we went to a spot ten leagues away where the savages thought there were deer in great numbers. Some twenty-five savages...went

into the woods near a little grove of firs where they made a triangular enclosure, closed on two sides, open on one. The enclosure was made of great wooden stakes eight or nine feet in height, joined close together, and the length of each side was nearly fifteen hundred paces. At the extremity of this triangle there is a little enclosure, getting narrower the farther it goes and partly covered with branches, with only one opening five feet wide, about the width of an average gate, by which the deer were to enter. They did this so well that in less than ten days their enclosure was ready...When everything was completed, they set out half an hour before daybreak to go into the woods about half a league from their enclosure, keeping about eighty paces apart, each having two sticks which they strike together, walking slowly in that forma-tion until they reach their enclosure. The deer, hearing this noise, flee before them until they reach the enclosure into which the savages force them to enter. Then the latter gradually coming together towards the opening of their triangle, the deer steal along the said palisades until they reach the extremity, whither the savages pursue them hotly with bow and arrow in hand, ready to shoot. And when the savages reach the extremity of their said triangle, they begin to shout and imitate the cry of wolves, whereof there are many that devour deer. The deer, hearing this terri-fying noise, are forced to enter the retreat by the small opening, whither they are very hotly

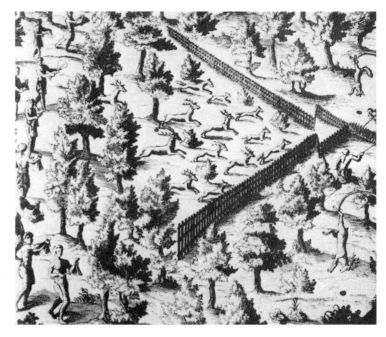

In 1615, French explorer Samuel de Champlain observed a band of Huron Indians hunting deer in the vicinity of Georgian Bay, Ontario. He sketched the sizeable V-shaped trap, built in less then 10 days by 25 braves, by which they managed to kill 120 deer in midautumn, when the animals were in hog-fat conditions for best venison. The ingenuity and resourcefulness of these hunters was remarkable, considering their crude tools. (The Champlain Society.)

pursued with arrows, and when they have entered, they are easily caught in this retreat, which is so well enclosed and barricaded that they can never get out of it. I assure you that one takes a peculiar pleasure in this mode of hunting, which took place every second day, and they did so well that in thirty-eight days that we were there [October 28 - December 4], they captured one hundred and twenty deer,

*with which they made good cheer, keeping the
fat for the winter and using it as we do butter,
and a little of the meat which they carry home
for their feasts."*

The deer hides were tanned for clothing and other purposes;
the fact is, of course, that the Indians used everything from
an animal except its "squeal."

# USE OF FIRE

Spring and summer fire-drives were commonly used by
some tribes to hunt game. Fire-surrounds were also
employed to take deer in autumn, when dry leaves and
grasses provided ready fuel. Deer were also driven onto a
narrow peninsula and thence into the water, and shot by
bow or speared either during the drive or from canoes in
cases of swimming animals trying to escape. One writer
noted that the Ojibway word for lake was *mitchigan*,
literally translated as "a wooden fence to catch deer near
its bank."

There is still controversy regarding how much impact
Indians had on Upper Midwest forests. Some investigators
believe that they cleared only a few areas of land (several
hundred acres) for villages, mound-building, and corn
fields, and set fires along the prairie/forest border to help
maintain the oak savanna along the edge of the Great
Plains. One anthropologist remarked that the
contention that burning by Indians was a major factor in
the ecology of Upper Great Lakes forests should be a matter
of investigation, not supposition. A valid point, but one that
is very difficult to document for lack of definitive evidence.
Available information, although largely circumstantial, suggests that fire indeed was routinely used by most Indians to
set back forest succession, thereby enhancing an area's
game carrying capacity, although there apparently were
considerable differences regarding when and how the burning
was done. In the northeastern states, forests that could be
burned easily were ignited by the largely nomadic Indians
to clear land for field crops, as protection against natural
fires, to control insects and snakes, stimulation of berry-
producing plants, for warfare and defense, for hunting,
maintenance of travel routes, and to increase or regenerate
forages attractive to game. The Ojibway surely must have
known about the practical benefits accruing from burning,
since they customarily traded (e.g., distinctive Keweenaw
copper) with tribes elsewhere that regularly used fire to
enhance their welfare. (Even the Aborigines of Australia —
primitive bushmen — have employed fire for such purposes
ever since they arrived on the sub-continent some 50,000
years ago. In fact, one researcher concluded that "it was fire
as much as social organization and stone tools that enabled
big game hunters to encircle the globe and to begin the
extermination of selected species.") Indians evidently had
little use for closed forests. One could speculate that their
deliberate, repeated burnings produced special "deserts", or
barrens (e.g., Lac Vieux Desert). The French word *brule*, a
common term in the Upper Great Lakes, means burnt, possibly in reference to Indian fire-created openings. Recent
investigation indicated that Indians periodically set fire to
pine-dominated (sandy) sites bordering Lake Superior within
what is now the Pictured Rocks National Lakeshore.
Presumably these burns were done to induce blueberry
production related to summer encampment.

Some forest types are better suited for burning than others. It probably was just a matter of waiting until ideal incendiary conditions prevailed; but Indians had plenty of time and patience for this. From a game production standpoint, the easiest and best areas to burn in the U.P. would have been the spruce-fir and hardwood/conifer stands, which then temporarily converted to the aspen type. Aspen is the staff of life for beaver, heavily browsed by deer and moose, and its male buds/catkins provide crucial winter nourishment for ruffed grouse. Fire triggers copious root-suckers in aspen, an effective means of clonal propagation. Aspen also is a prolific seed producer, and its "cotton" is readily blown many miles by wind. Hence it is well adapted to seeding-in on fresh ash on moist sites after a fire. The typical open canopy of aspen stands enables a variety of sun-loving plants to grow in the understory. The seeds of many pioneer species (e.g. raspberry) seem to be waiting for the heat of a scorching fire (or unshaded sun) to germinate, after lying dormant for years under a few inches of accumulated leaf litter and duff. Such fire-dependent, secondary succession plants usually grow lush, and the fruits of some species provide nutritious fare for sundry wildlife, as well as humans. (Because moose and caribou — unlike white-tailed deer —rarely browse white cedar, Indians would have gained little by setting fire to conifer swamps, which periodically burned naturally anyway.)

# THE SAVAGE LAND

Prehistoric Indian populations in the Upper Great Lakes undoubtedly were low because these people could barely survive in this rigorous, inhospitable region. Contrary to popular belief, the land was not teaming with game; winters were so severe that populations of moose, caribou, and deer fluctuated drastically from year to year. Indians did not live for a whole year in the same place, since they had to keep moving to new grounds to find enough food to stay alive. Their societies were divided into bands, villages, clans, and families. Each of the many bands had its own hunting and fishing territory. A band numbering 600 might occupy a 1,200 square mile area. In autumn they split up into families, each using its traditional hunting grounds. Early spring was the most critical period for obtaining food. Although all cervids were then in poorest physical condition, and therefore easiest to bring down, hunting was then also the most difficult. The best strategy for survival was to remain relatively inactive so as to reduce expenditure of vital energy (a trick learned by whitetails eons earlier to good advantage). However, some authorities contend that Indians resorted to group hunting in spring, since the "communal effort of a tribe was then needed to replenish exhausted [food] resources," thereby preventing catastrophic starvation.

The best "guesstimate" as to the number of Indians in and around Lake Superior when the white man arrived is 20,000 -25,000, or about one person per two square miles on average. Their densities doubtless were much lower along the frigid snowy shore of Superior than in the warmer clime farther south. Of this number, the Ojibway population probably numbered approximately 4,500. A Wisconsin biologist concluded that at no time did that state have more than 10,000 Indians, a density which averages out at one person per five square miles. But this includes the lower part of Wisconsin, where, as in southern Michigan, climatic conditions for human habitation were much more tolerable than in the northern tier. The 1840 census showed there were only 1,000 Indians (probably including mixed-bloods) living in the U.P., an average of one person per 16 square miles. Although emigration may account in part for this unexpectedly low density, a more plausible explanation is that this was the region's true carrying capacity for Indians, particularly after their game supply was seriously depleted with the advent of the fur trade. Longfellow poignantly describes the dreadful aftermath of a cold, cruel winter with ever thicker ice and ever deeper snow:

> *Hardly from his buried wigwam*
> *Could the hunter force a passage;*
> *With his mittens and his snow-shoes*
> *Vainly walked he through the forest,*
> *Sought for bird or beast and found none,*
> *Saw no track of deer or rabbit,*
> *In the snow beheld no footprints,*
> *In the ghastly, gleaming forest*
> *Fell, and could not rise from weakness,*
> *Perished there from cold and hunger.*

> *Oh the famine and the fever!*

Not even the indomitable Hiawatha could find enough game to keep his wife from starving. In desperation he implored Gitche Manitou, the Mighty, for deliverance:

> *Give your children food, O father!*
> *Give us food, or we must perish!*
> *Give me food for Minnehaha,*
> *For my dying Minnehaha!*

But his pleading was to no avail:

> *Then they buried Minnehaha;*
> *In the snow a grave they made her,*
> *In the forest deep and darksome,*
> *Underneath the moaning hemlocks;*
> *Clothed her in her richest garments,*
> *Wrapped her in her robes of ermine,*
> *Covered her with snow, like ermine;*

Famine has other, more insidious effects on human demographics. As in all mammals, food shortage in young women delays the onset of puberty (menarche), and extreme fasting suppresses ovulation. A women's fertility pattern closely depends upon the amount of body fat present at a given time. A comparatively high level of circulating lipids from ample deposits (i.e. a high fat:lean biomass ratio) signals to her endocrine system that the prospects for successful reproduction are favorable at that moment. At the dawn of civilization this condition might have ensued from feasting on a mastodon or two, for instance, which the clan had fortuitously killed or which had died accidentally. (By the Late Woodland period, however, reliance on stored crops and exploitation of spring fish runs led to a dramatic increase in human fecundity due to greater population carrying capacity for a unit of land.) Similarly, prenatal and neonatal mortality would be a direct outcome of severe malnutrition during pregnancy and early lactation, respectively. Infant losses almost certainly ran high in most tribes, and would help explain the "loose Indian code of sex morality which permitted and encouraged promiscuity." Such sexual activity might have constituted an effort on a woman's part to eventually bear a live child and nurse it in good health to weaning age, an overwhelming maternal aspiration. (Ironically, advent of a sedentary existence evidently generated higher infant mortality and reduced life expectancy, "presumably in response to increased infectious disease resulting from more crowded and less sanitary living conditions.")

# SPIRITUAL CODES

Hunting was a very important part of a brave's life. Next to warfare and attending council, it enjoyed the greatest prestige. Hunting was arduous and time-consuming work, however, and it could not be considered a sport in any real sense. Indians viewed wildlife as their spiritual or ecological kin. Killing of animals, while not taboo, was done only as needed, and with proper atonement for the act. A scarcity of game was viewed as a consequence of a sacred misdeed which a hunter must reconcile with the Great Spirit. Because their very lives depended upon a reliable game supply, Indians assiduously conserved (i.e. managed) their wildlife resources. There simply was no reason for them to kill more animals than needed for immediate use. Some meat was converted into pemmican or jerky for the coming winter if a surplus was harvested, but none was wasted. Killing of young animals was strictly prohibited by most (but apparently not all) tribes.

Hunters intimately knew the game resources of their ancestral territory. Encroachment on one's traditional hunting grounds by another tribe was just cause for immediate retaliation, namely war. One report noted that warfare between members of opposing tribes in Minnesota in effect prevented the competing hunters from utilizing a "no-man's-land" between their adjacent territories. This action tended to preserve game populations within these overlapping buffer zones, or de facto sanctuaries. (A striking parallel was reported for wolves, who must respect the territorial integrity of rival packs, thereby providing a refuge for their normal prey, e.g., deer, residing within the boundaries of these uncontested sites.)

# TRIALS AND TRIBULATIONS

Unfortunately, the "benign symbiosis" that originally existed between Indians and wildlife radically changed after Europeans came on the scene. The Indians soon abandoned their spiritual bonds and taboos concerning harvesting of game and furbearers, and began to seriously overexploit them. Among numerous examples, one settler wrote that during a particularly severe winter in northern Wisconsin in 1857, white men and Indians slaughtered deer in great numbers: "They would put on snowshoes and, taking a hatchet but no gun, would strike them down. The snow was crusted and would bear a man's weight, but the deer, falling through, would be so crippled in their traveling that they were easily caught." One pioneer reported killing 10 deer in one day, but in some places the Indians had taken them by the hundreds. Not surprisingly, deer were scarce there the next year. Writers frequently mentioned that game increased substantially after Indians left an area or were confined to reservations.

What compelled the Indians to go on such a killing frenzy? Quite likely there were a number of reasons, none of which in itself is altogether a persuasive answer. One logical explanation is simply that of greed — if you can't fight the white man, join him! According to wildlife biologists Richard and Thomas McCabe, in this setting, game animals and furbearers "were reduced to a commodity, with Indians acting as the white merchant's functionary in a three-century spate of exploitation that left the land nearly barren of certain wildlife and the Indians themselves destitute of subsistence and cultural options." After they acquired steel traps and muskets, the Indians sold or bartered countless millions of deerskins and pelts of beaver and other valuable furs, a slaughter aided and abetted by conniving traders in expectation of rich profits.

The literature is replete with tales about how the Indians were supplied rum or brandy and then swindled out of their precious fur catch upon reaching a drunken stupor on the fire-water. Frequently they became "howling drunk," a scary sordid spectacle that sometimes lasted several days and involved an entire village. Why were these people seemingly constitutionally unable to handle liquor? For millennia the Indians drank only water, unlike the Caucasians who had imbibed beer and wine since long before biblical times. It has therefore been hypothesized that in their evolution the Indians did not develop a genetic tolerance for alcohol, i.e., they lacked a physiologic ability to promptly metabolize it into harmless by-products. Hence they readily became inebriated and addicted to this foreign substance.[2] It is well known, of course, that Indians had little or no natural immunity against the so-called "white man's diseases" like smallpox, measles, typhoid, and other scourges, and whole tribes were ravaged by virulent epidemics of these intro-duced maladies. Conversely, however, there is evidence to indicate that in return the Indians transmitted syphilis and other infectious diseases to genetically susceptible whites,

A bronzed Father Marquette surveils his namesake city on the south shore of Lake Superior. The renowned Black-Robed priest established several missions in the Upper Great Lakes area, most notably the one at St. Ignace, Michigan (which he named in honor of the Jesuit Society's founder). He died in 1672 near what is now the Pere Marquette River, which empties into Lake Michigan. Two years later his Indian converts brought Marquette's mortal remains to the St. Ignace mission for interment in the church graveyard. His burial site is marked with a modest monument for such an esteemed personage. This idealized statue was designed by Gaetano Trentanove of Florence, Italy, in 1897. A replica, in marble, stands in the Nation's Capitol.

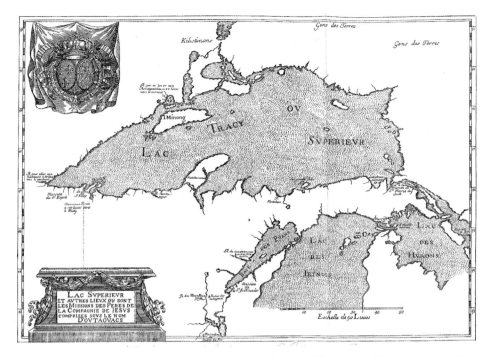

*The intrepid missionary/explorer Jacques Marquette, aided by Father Claude Jean Allouez (or vice versa), prepared this extraordinarily accurate map of Upper Michigan. It was published in the Jesuit Relations in 1672, but credited to Claude Dablon, their superior. Accompanied by Louis Joliet, Father Marquette canoed up the Fox River from Green Bay, made a short portage to the Wisconsin River, thence floated downstream to its confluence with the Mississippi, thus becoming the first (recorded) whites to view the mighty river since De Soto, 130 years before. (Burrows Brothers.)*

beginning with Columbus' first voyage to the New World.[3]

The Ojibway must have experienced profound spiritual and cultural shock when the Jesuit missionaries began arriving from France in 1641 at Sault Ste. Marie. These intrepid priests, called the Black-Robes by the Indians, were as intent on scientific discovery and exploration as in saving the souls of the pagan natives. They were, nonetheless, extremely fervent (even fanatical) in fulfilling the Lord's sacramental edict to the Apostles: "go ... and make disciples of all the nations" (Matt. 28/16-20). The Judeo-Christian concept of sin and contrite repentance for esoteric wickedness must have come as a jolt to these fearless, self-reliant people who had their own code of ethics and religion. Initially, at least, the Black-Robes and Indians did not get along well. In going from Sault Ste. Marie to L'Anse in 1660, for instance, Father Rene

Menard "found himself among savages who were in the depths of irritation, profanity and hate. They had not heard about God; they wanted no prayer, no discipline, no advice. Quickly they let the priest know that his way of life was resented here." To what extent conversion to Christianity (and its puritanical mores) subverted the Indians' traditional respect for wildlife is conjecture. One would suspect that these proud people suffered severe psychotrauma — a crushing loss of identity and self-esteem — in the process of embracing an alien God. Longfellow alludes to impending trouble in Paradise. After learning why the Black-Robes had come to his land, and while these guests were still slumbering in his wigwam, the noble chieftain Hiawatha told old Nokomis, without elucidation, that he was going on a long and distant journey in his canoe. His people gathered by the shore, wailing "farewell forever" as he sailed away.

> Thus deported Hiawatha,
> Hiawatha the Beloved,
> In the glory of the sunset,
> In the purple mists of evening,
> To the regions of the home-wind,
> Of the Northwest-Wind Keewaydin,
> To the Islands of the Blessed,
> To the Kingdom of Ponemah,
> To the Land of the Hereafter!

Some Indians, to wit the Tlingit of Alaska, commit suicide by going to sea in a canoe *sans* paddle. Maybe after divining the future, and disliking what he saw as inevitable, this was Hiawatha's intention; a way of reaching the tribe's Happy Hunting Grounds and meeting his venerable ancestors. Schoolcraft noted that Indians did not regard the

*Legend has it that Father Marquette preached Christianity to Ojibways seated in canoes at a place now known as Chapel Rock, midway between Munising and Grand Marais. Today this inspiring stretch of beach is scoured by "rockhounds" searching for the elusive semi-precious Lake Superior agate. (Michigan Department Conservation.)*

approach of death with horror; being deists in religion, they looked upon it as a change of state, which was mainly for the better.

# THEIR FINEST HOUR

Although the Ojibway were not particularly war-like, the men were nevertheless fierce warriors when the occasion demanded. According to Chase and Stellanova Osborn, a ferocious battle with the invading Six-Nation Iroquois in 1662 was the turning point in Ojibway history — the greatest single achievement of the tribe — when they annihilated the enemy at a cape of land on Whitefish Bay, less than 20 miles west of Sault Ste. Marie, since known, appropriately, as Iroquois Point. The Iroquois,

An isolated lighthouse on Whitefish Bay west of Sault Ste. Marie marks the spot where local Indian warriors courageously annihilated a marauding war-party of ferocious Iroquois. The aboriginal name for this point of land, appropriately enough, means the "place of Iroquois bones", because their skeletons were left to bleach along the shoreline after the heroic battle.

"after a victorious onslaught on the Ojibway, encamped, a thousand strong, upon this point, where, thinking themselves secure, they made a war-feast to torture and devour their prisoners. Their orgies rose to heights of wild delirium such that only Indians can create. The Chippewas, beholding the humiliation and suffering of their brethren from the opposite shore, were roused to sudden fury. Collecting their warriors, only three hundred in all, they crossed the channel, and at break of day fell upon the Iroquois, then sleeping after their horrible excesses. Tradition says that they massacred all the Iroquois — men, women, and children — except two, and stuck their heads on stakes which they imbedded in the ground at intervals for some miles above the point. The bones were left to bleach on the shore."

*Renowned artist Frederic Remington painted this tranquil scene of Radisson and Groseilliers on their trailblazing canoe trip around Lake Superior in 1659-60. These daring explorers initiated the fabulous fur trade in the Northwest, headquartered at Montreal. (Buffalo Bill Historical Center, gift of Mrs. Karl Frank.)*

# 4

# THE FUR TRADE

Although Etienne Brule, one of Samuel de Champlain's scouts, discovered Lake Superior around 1615, and Jean Nicolet was the first white to see Lake Michigan in 1634, the French-Canadian fur trade in the Upper Great Lakes did not actually begin until 1659. In that year Pierre Esprit Radisson and his brother-in-law Sieur des Groseilliers (nee Medard Chouart) left Three Rivers, Quebec, in August and headed via the Ottawa River/French River/St. Marys River route for Lake Superior. They proceeded along the south shore of Superior in their canoes, wintered at the southwestern end of it, and returned via the northern route in 1660. They came back from this circumnavigation with a fortune in furs — thousands of pelts, enough to fill 60 cargo canoes! But because they had left clandestinely, minus official sanction, both men were arrested and fined upon return, and their furs confiscated. Disgruntled, they turned to the British, who had previously laid claim to the Hudson Bay region, to exploit the potentially lucrative fur trade in the then still vaguely defined Northwest Territory. The Hudson's Bay Company thus was chartered in 1670, with outposts at Fort Albany and Moose Factory on James Bay.

## THE *COUREURS DES BOIS*

Without their king's permission — indeed despite a death sentence from France to do so — Quebec colonists pursued the fur trade vigorously as individual entrepreneurs soon becoming known as *coureurs des bois*, literally woods-runners. Later, after receiving royal blessing of a sort, the fur trade continued until New France was lost to rival England, who won the French and Indian War in 1763. The British were slow to take advantage of this dispossession, however; in 1765 only one of its employees (Alexander Henry) was granted a license to trade for furs, at the Fort Michilimackinac post on the south side of the Straits of Mackinac. In 1779 a group of canny Scotsmen led by Simon McTavish organized the North West Company, known as the "Nor'westers," which paralleled and competed with the Hudson's Bay Company to the north. The North West Company led in the Lake Superior fur trade for more than 40 years. Because of unscrupulous dealings and often vicious head-to-head altercations, the two companies were forced to merge in 1821, keeping the Hudson's Bay name. In 1808 John Jacob Astor joined the fray by establishing the upstart American Fur Company, with a trading post as far west as Astoria, Oregon, at the mouth of the Columbia River. After the Revolutionary War, and after the attendant boundary dispute with Canada had

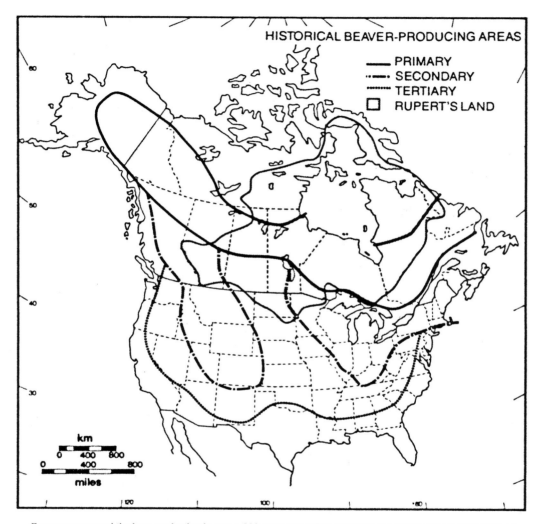

HISTORICAL BEAVER-PRODUCING AREAS

——— PRIMARY
—·—· SECONDARY
········ TERTIARY
□ RUPERT'S LAND

*Europeans pursued the beaver relentlessly over a 300-year span (1550-1850) because its fur was in great demand for making felt hats. Although indigenous to all of North America, the historical primary range based on the animal's relative abundance and fur quality was north of the contiguous United States, mainly in the aspen parklands of the Canadian prairie. (Ontario Ministry Natural Resources.)*

*French-Canadian voyageurs moved people and exchanged trade goods for furs between Montreal and trading posts such as at Grand Portage, Minnesota, via birchbark canoes requiring 8-9 paddlers. Smaller canoes were used on the shallower waterways leading to remote hinterlands. These hardy workers ideally were less than five feet six inches tall to save precious cargo weight. Though small in size, they reputedly could tote two 90-pound packs or fur bales at a trot around a portage. Passengers rarely substituted for payload, as shown here. (National Archives Canada.)*

been resolved, the American Fur Company gained control of all former North West Company trading posts on the U.S. side of its new border, including the one at Grand Portage, Minnesota. In 1803, the North West Company moved its headquarters to the mouth of the Kaministiquia River, at Fort William, Ontario. The American Fur Company also used the St. Louis River route, near Fond du Lac, Minnesota, to reach the Rainy River and Mississippi,

respectively. When Astor retired in 1834, what was left of the Michigan fur trade collapsed soon thereafter.

According to historian Ida Johnson: "From the beginning of the fur trade regime to its close a bitter warfare was waged for the possession of this 'golden fleece' of the New World; monopolizing companies competed with the coureurs des bois, Indian tribe with Indian tribe, French

*The awesome rapids of Saint Marys River (Sault Ste. Marie) drop 20 feet in a mile in draining the Lake Superior watershed. The famed "Soo" locks, constructed in 1855, allowed ships to circumvent the former arduous portage at this site. The present flow is only a trickle compared to its former volume, as most of the water has been siphoned off for commercial ventures. Historically important as an Indian fishery, anglers with modern tackle now wade the shallows on the Canadian side of the river, often using dry-flies to lure huge trout.*

*Although the flotilla of fur-trader canoes no longer ply the French River emptying into Georgian Bay, in Lake Huron, they have been replaced by recreational crafts paddled by persons who enjoy the ambiance of this historic waterway. A prominent sign now warns canoers of dangerous falls ahead.*

with English, English with American, independent trader with trading companies, and vice versa. It was a competition that lasted until the forest was stripped of its rich supply of peltries."

In its heyday the North West Company's fur trading route extended some 3,000 miles, from Montreal on the St. Lawrence River to as far north as Great Slave Lake, with side trips up the Athabasca and Saskatchewan Rivers. The route included more than 100 portages, some up to 13 miles long, the most famous being the one by-passing the Pigeon River rapids at Grand Portage, Minnesota, near the western tip of Lake Superior. The all-important site at Grand Portage, the annual summer *rendezvous* or "meeting place," was first used by the coureurs des bois and Jesuit missionaries sometime after 1722, and by the Nor'westers from 1784 to 1803. The early French *voyageurs* (travelers) consisted of two distinct groups. The Montreal men, derisively called *mangeur de lard*, or pork-eaters, traveled to Grand Portage in large birch bark canoes *(canot du maitre)* about 36 feet long and 6 feet wide, capable of hauling up to 8,000 pounds of cargo and paddled by 8 or 9 men. Smaller canoes, 25 feet long, were used on narrow, shallow watercourses to reach the remote hinterlands. These *canot du nord* were paddled by 4 - 6 men known as winterers, but also called *hivernauts*, or old-hands, because they were expert woodsmen. The coureurs des bois and voyageurs (names ultimately used synonymously) reputedly led a short, happy life — greatly romanticized — being particularly subject to accidents and disease incurred by their enervating, danger-prone existence. Ida Johnson opined that the coureur des bois was a "prideful and debasing social outcast of New France who foisted his fur-trade thievery and depravity on helpless Indians." Their reputation for drunkenness and lechery doubtless was well-earned.

At peak there were some 2,000 men roaming the north country in the fur trade. The lure for this feverish activity was the beaver, whose pelage was in great demand for making gentlemen's felt hats, then in high fashion in Europe. Although beaver were found throughout North America, the mother-lode in their abundance was the aspen parklands in and around the Canadian prairie. Aspen, their staple diet, was plentiful here, and the sluggish streams in this region could be readily dammed.

Winters at that latitude are prolonged and frigid, hence beaver pelts "primed" early in the season with thick under-fur to ward off the bitter cold.

Beavers were the coin-of-the-realm until the early 1800s. The Indians were eager to trap them; one skin would buy a kettle, a blanket was worth six pelts, while 12 beaver could be traded for a gun. The Indians also trapped other furbearers, of course; ermine (weasel) was in demand by English royalty for ceremonial robes, the rich wanted lynx skins for bed covers, and marten (sable), otter, and mink were fancied by ladies for luxurious coats.

*In 1715, French soldiers constructed Fort St. Philippe de Michilimackinac on the south shore of the Straits, across from short-lived Fort de Baude near St. Ignace. It soon became a major fur-trading center, first under New France rule and later (1761) under the British until the garrison moved to Fort Mackinac in 1781. Today reconstructed Fort Michilimackinac is best known as the site of the infamous massacre of its British soldiers in 1763 by wily Chippewa warriors during what is known as Pontiac's Rebellion, named after the Ottawa chief who attacked Detroit.*

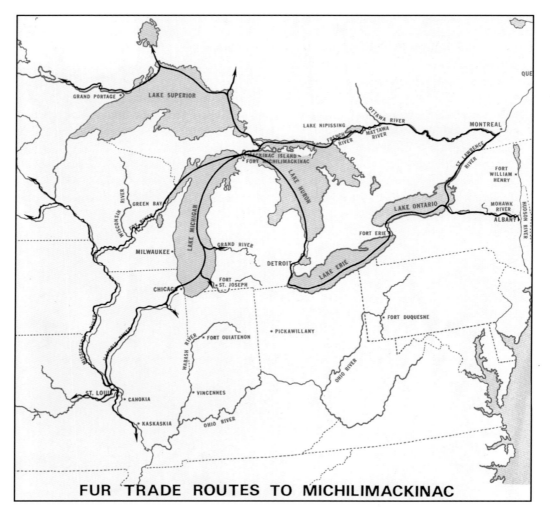

## FUR TRADE ROUTES TO MICHILIMACKINAC

*Fort Michilimackinac served as a focal point for fur-trading operations spanning an immense region, and therefore did not solely reflect Michigan's contribution of pelts. In 1778 alone, "128 canoes brought over 2,100 kegs of rum and brandy, 1,500 muskets, 28 tons of gun powder, 33 tons of shot and ball, and hundreds of bales of trade goods to be exchanged for furs." In return, countless pelts from remote regions were shipped to Montreal for export to Europe. (Mackinac State Historic Parks.)*

# Michigan Fur Records (or Lack Thereof)

Because of its strategic location, Sault Ste. Marie was the first to assume importance as a fur trading center in Upper Michigan. By 1689, however, it was practically abandoned, and Fort Michilimackinac grew to greater prominence. Unfortunately, it is impossible to estimate the amount and value of Upper Michigan's fur take during the Seventeenth and Eighteenth Centuries because pelts brought to the Sault and Michilimackinac posts were not representative of those caught locally, since many skins came from the uncharted wilderness of the Canadian provinces, as well as from Illinois, Wisconsin, and even beyond the Mississippi River. The French trader as a rule was not a man of letters, and left no account of his wanderings. Much of our knowledge about the early fur trade had to be gleaned from the missionaries' chronicles in the *Jesuit Relations And Allied Documents*. The early fur trader was concerned mainly with beaver pelts, but one account book for 1796 ambiguously reported that "99 packs were sold, composed of 5 bears, 5 beaver, 10 fishers, 58 cats, 74 doe, 78 foxes, 108 wolves, 117 otters, 183 mink, 557 bucks, 1,231 deer, 1,340 muskrats, and 5,582 raccoons." Ada Johnson noted that most of the ledgers for the American Fur Company kept at Mackinac Island were destroyed: "In 1836 several boxes of these [account] books were opened and the contents used for lighting fires, etc."

Given these fragmentary and equivocal records, it is hopeless to try to reconstruct the true nature of furbearer populations in the U.P. in the early trading days. Records

*Beginning in 1784, the North West Company's Simon McTavish and fellow Scotsmen ran the fur trading post/fort at Grand Portage, Minnesota. Each year in July, voyageurs from Montreal arrived for their annual rendezvous with canoers from the Canadian wilderness to barter furs for trade goods. The latter had to bypass a stretch of rapids on the Pigeon River, a 9-mile trek, with heavily laden packs. The reconstructed stockade and main buildings (e.g., the Great Hall) at the historic Grand Portage site have been designated a National Monument.*

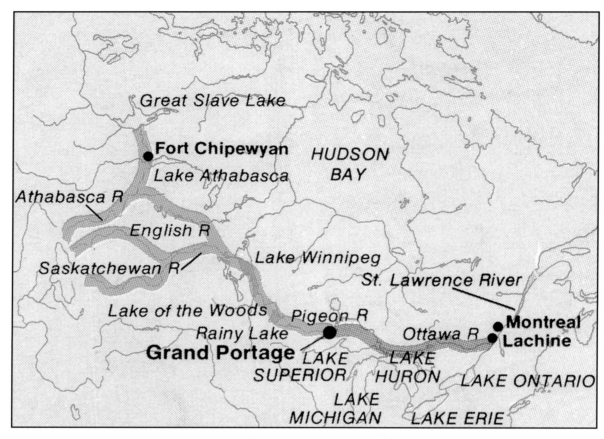

*From 1784 to 1803, North West Company fur traders paddled cargo canoes from Montreal to Grand Portage (orange), thence in smaller craft to as far north as Great Slave Lake and environs (green); a route totalling some 3,000 miles long. (National Park Service.)*

for the 1800s in particular would be quite useless as to primeval wildlife status, since by then forest habitats had been altered drastically by settlers, with some species reduced to a fraction of their former abundance; the dire consequence of the credo — "kill as long as there is something left to kill!"

# WHAT MEANT WHAT

Among the many difficulties encountered in trying to piece together accurate details of the early fur trade is the problem of semantics. Michigan biologist Paul Hickie astutely deduced that available original records frequently suffered from misidentification of New World animals, as well as that of misnomers. For example, in the Great Lakes region the range of moose, elk, caribou, and deer tended to overlap. The name of each species, and of deer in general — common and technical in both French and English — was loosely used and interchangeable. The result has been a confused jumble of names often incorrectly interpreted. For example, the French called the American moose *elan*, their word for elk, because that is what the European moose was labelled. The trouble began when persons traveling south of moose range encountered elk, which looked so large in comparison with deer that they also called these animals elk, which was technically but not linguistically correct. Translators of French documents about the New World frequently ignored the differences in nomenclature, so that in many instances elan was construed to mean elk when it should actually have signified moose. A serious error of this type was evident in the translations of a French trader-trapper's memoirs which told of Indians snaring more than 2,400 elans on Manitoulin Island (in northern Lake Huron) in the winter of 1670-71. Hickie concluded that careful reading of the original document indicated that the interchangeable term referred to moose; besides, the area lies too far north to have been elk range. (On the other hand, a Canadian biologist later reasoned that the animal in question actually was the caribou. This makes sense, since Manitoulin Island isn't large enough to support such a huge moose population, whereas caribou were migratory, rather than resident year round.)

Jacques Cartier, on his voyage up the St. Lawrence River in 1545, reported "a great store of Stags Deere, Beares, and other like sorts of beasts...." Stags Deere in this case probably referred to bull elk, the American equivalent of the European red deer. White-tailed deer were also known colloquially as Virginia deer, common deer, jumping deer, long-tailed deer, bannertail, flag-tailed deer, fallow deer (a different animal, albeit with fawn-spotted pelage), or roe deer (a much smaller European cervid). Many early accounts or translations simply cited the word *deer* without further identification. Hence a "red deer" could denote elk, or merely an adult whitetail in summer coat.

What were game populations in the Upper Great Lakes roughly like when the French arrived? Radisson told about seeing (and killing) a *oriniack*, the Indian word for moose, during his exploration of the south shore of Lake Superior. He noted that "the bears, the castors [beavers], and the Oriniack showed themselves often, but to their great cost; indeed it was to us like a terrestrial paradise after such a long fasting, and such great labors, to find ourselves able

*This primitive cabin, built on Grand Island in the early 1830's, served for many years as a trading post for the American Fur Company. It was moved across the bay to Munising for safekeeping as an historic artifact. A companion cabin reposes in the Michigan State University museum at East Lansing. Company officials complained that Abraham Williams, the first white settler on Grand Island, was illegally trading whiskey to the Indians, but they nonetheless soon joined him in such spirited competition for local furs.*

to choose our own diet..." Near present-day Ashland, Wisconsin, Radisson wrote in his journal: "Then I killed an Oriniack. I could have killed more but we liked the [water] fowles better." Some years later, at the headwaters of the Chippewa River in Wisconsin, he related: "We killed several other beasts, as Oriniacks, caribou, fallow does and bucks [elk], Catts of mountain [mountain lions], child of the Devill [wolverines]; in a word, we led a good life." Engrossing reading to be sure, but hardly a very useful census of wildlife abundance at the beginning of recorded history in the New World. Lest the reader be badly mislead, Radisson also told of "great hunger" they endured when game and fish were scarce or unavailable because of early or unusually heavy snowfall. In several instances conditions were so bad that they were forced to eat roots, leather, or even their dogs to keep from starving. He and his companions mostly ate well because they could waylay unwary animals at long range with muskets.

*The tradition of canoe travel fostered by the fur trade lives on as a tranquil form of recreation among aficionados.*
*The canvas-covered craft used here is not basically different from the paper birch-clad type devised centuries ago by regional Indians.*

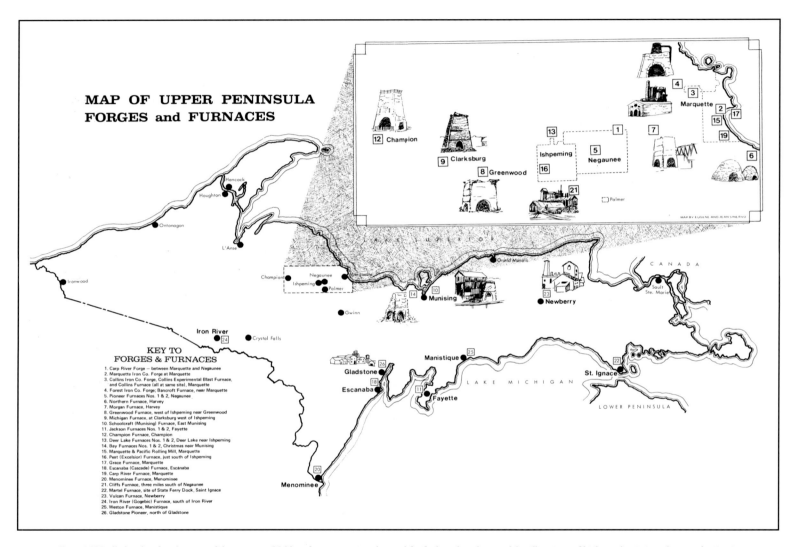

# MAP OF UPPER PENINSULA
# FORGES and FURNACES

12 Champion

9 Clarksburg

8 Greenwood

13 Ishpeming 16

1

5 Negaunee

7

21

☐ Palmer

4

3

Marquette

2

15 17

19

6

MAP BY EUGENE AND JEAN SINERVO

Hancock

Haughton

Ontonagon

L'Anse

Ironwood

LAKE SUPERIOR

Grand Marais

CANADA

Champion
Ishpeming
Negaunee
Marquette
Palmer

Gwinn

14 10 Munising

23 Newberry

Sault Ste. Marie

Iron River
24

Crystal Falls

25 Manistique

22 St. Ignace

Gladstone
26

LAKE MICHIGAN

LOWER PENINSULA

Escanaba 18

11 Fayette

20

Menominee

## KEY TO
## FORGES & FURNACES
1. Carp River Forge — between Marquette and Negaunee
2. Marquette Iron Co. Forge at Marquette
3. Collins Iron Co. Forge, Collins Experimental Blast Furnace, and Collins Furnace (all at same site), Marquette
4. Forest Iron Co. Forge; Bancroft Furnace, near Marquette
5. Pioneer Furnaces Nos. 1 & 2, Negaunee
6. Northern Furnace, Harvey
7. Morgan Furnace, Harvey
8. Greenwood Furnace, west of Ishpeming near Greenwood
9. Michigan Furnace, at Clarksburg west of Ishpeming
10. Schoolcraft (Munising) Furnace, East Munising
11. Jackson Furnaces Nos. 1 & 2, Fayette
12. Champion Furnace, Champion
13. Deer Lake Furnaces Nos. 1 & 2, Deer Lake near Ishpeming
14. Bay Furnaces Nos. 1 & 2, Christmas near Munising
15. Marquette & Pacific Rolling Mill, Marquette
16. Peat (Excelsior) Furnace, just south of Ishpeming
17. Grace Furnace, Marquette
18. Escanaba (Cascade) Furnace, Escanaba
19. Carp River Furnace, Marquette
20. Menominee Furnace, Menominee
21. Cliffs Furnace, three miles south of Negaunee
22. Martel Furnace, site of State Ferry Dock, Saint Ignace
23. Vulcan Furnace, Newberry
24. Iron River (Gogebic) Furnace, south of Iron River
25. Weston Furnace, Manistique
26. Gladstone Pioneer, north of Gladstone

*From 1858 till shortly after the turn of the century, 28 blast furnaces using charcoal for fuel produced around 2 million tons of high-grade pig iron. Iron production in the U. P. was a far-flung operation, as indicated by the furnace locations. Several sites also housed experimental forges, and one furnace (Excelsior) tried using peat to smelt the ore. (Northern Michigan University Press.)*

# 5

# CLEARCUT AND BURN

For approximately the first 200 years of European activity in Michigan, their direct impact on the landscape was comparatively slight. However, the situation changed tremendously with the discovery of iron ore in 1844 near Teal Lake (on the Marquette Range) and with the advent of intensive copper mining in the Keweenaw Peninsula (Cliff Lode) at about the same time. Prospectors and mine workers swarmed into these areas to gain their fair share of the promised riches. Soon the city of Calumet had the largest population in Michigan; Marquette increased from 1,000 persons in 1860 to 4,000 in the next census ten years later. By 1873, Ishpeming ("Hell Town") had a population of 6,000.

The mass copper in the Keweenaw range was essentially pure in composition; thus it had only to be extracted from the ground and melted into ingots for the metal to be shipped to manufacturers downstate. In contrast, only the best iron ore contained less than 50 percent impurities; this waste had to be removed for efficient ship transportation to population centers southward, made possible by completion of the "Soo" locks, circumventing the St. Marys rapids, in 1855. (Later on some iron was shipped from ports on Lake Michigan.)

## CHARCOAL AND PIG IRON

The conventional strategy to produce usable iron was to smelt the ore in a blast furnace to yield a refined product called pig iron, so named because its castings resembled a litter of suckling piglets. In lieu of coke from coal, the fuel of choice (necessity) was charcoal, which could be made from the seemingly inexhaustible supply of timber in the surrounding forests. (According to Kenneth LaFayette, in England the charcoal-fired iron furnaces had used up practically the entire country's hardwood timber by the 1700s.) The trick to making charcoal is to heat wood, cut to suitable size, in a kiln in which combustion can be carefully controlled to drive off the volatile hydrocarbon gases. The end-product is charcoal, an amorphous form of carbon, which burns extremely hot under the air draft of a blast furnace. The best wood for making charcoal is sugar maple, followed by yellow birch and beech — all common components of a northern hardwood forest. However, about one-third of the furnaces used charcoal from white pine, hemlock, or whatever softwoods (conifers) were readily available. It is said that about 110 bushels of the best hardwood charcoal were required to smelt a ton of iron ore versus 140 bushels of conifer charcoal. In 1863,

*The Schoolcraft Iron Company blast furnace was constructed in East Munising in 1868. It ceased operations less than 10 years later for lack of charcoal fuel, after having consumed the timber from 40,000 acres of old growth northern hardwoods the company owned in the vicinity. Five kilns built at the furnace site, and six more several miles away (plus an additional 150 charcoal "pits") were constructed to fuel this facility. Munising Falls is faintly visible in the denuded background, having been rerouted (temporarily) along the escarpment from its original picturesque site for industrial purposes. (Marquette County Historical Society.)*

woodchoppers earned 75 - 80 cents a cord, measuring 4 x 4 x 8 feet, for bolts delivered to nearby kilns or charcoal "pits."[4] An acre of good hardwood could yield 35 cords of wood, each of which might produce 45 bushels of charcoal, or slightly over 1,500 bushels per acre. This reportedly was enough to smelt 14 tons of iron ore. Another authority stated, however, that an acre of timber yielded 30 cords of wood, which was converted to 1,000 bushels of charcoal, making enough fuel to produce 5 tons of iron. The latter figure most likely represented the average situation, taking into account the many variables (e.g, forest composition, ore quality and processing method, etc.) on iron tonnage.

At peak iron production (Civil War period), there were 28 blast furnaces, counting twin stacks, in operation in the U.P., half of them located in Marquette County. As the forest in the vicinity of an iron mine was eliminated, new ore bodies were discovered, and furnace operations were

*Only a relic structure marks the former iron-producing community of Onota (now Bay Furnace). The town burned to the ground in 1877 when a glowing ember ignited a wagonload of charcoal being brought in to fuel the blast furnace. The residents moved to another charcoal-producing site, also called Onota, in west Alger County; it too became a ghost town when the hardwood timber was cut out.*

*Hundreds of huge bee-hive shaped kilns were constructed across much of the region to produce the charcoal needed to fire the blast furnaces in making pig iron. They frequently were placed next to a hill to facilitate loading of the wood from the top. These relic charcoal kilns were built at the mouth of the Carp River south of Marquette. The hematite ore often was hauled long distances to blast furnaces located to take advantage of locally abundant hardwoods.*

shifted accordingly. It was cheaper to bring the heavy ore to the kilns than to transport the light but bulky charcoal to the mines. Thus iron smelting was done as far east as St. Ignace, westward to Iron River, and as far south as Menominee. The extensive hardwood forests near Munising attracted two major furnaces, one just east of town (Schoolcraft Furnace) and the other, with twin stacks, several miles westward at a settlement called Onota (now Bay Furnace). In less than 10 years, beginning in 1868, the Schoolcraft unit evidently burned enough charcoal to eliminate 40,000 acres of local timber. At Onota, woods roads fanned out to six sets of beehive-shaped kilns to supply the enormous amount of charcoal required for that operation. In 1872, about 3,500 cords of wood (2:1 hardwood/hemlock) were cut monthly from the nearby 20,000 acres of company land that horseshoed the smelters. Converting this forest to charcoal required 50 - 100 men. After the facility burned to the ground (via a smoldering ember in a wagonload of charcoal), in 1882 a new town of Onota was built 25 miles west of Munising near the Detroit, Mackinac, and Marquette Railroad tracks. Here 40 kilns were in operation before it, too, became a ghost town for lack of fuel. One entrepreneur (the "charcoal king") contracted to supply charcoal from Alger County, mainly for furnaces in Marquette and Iron County; in just one month in 1886, his crews cut 2,300 cords of wood, which meant razing about 66 acres of timber.

*In its 24 years of operation, blast furnaces at Fayette, nestled on Snail Shell Harbor in Lake Michigan, produced nearly 230,000 tons of high-grade pig iron. The townsite was built specifically for this venture, and in the 1880's housed over 500 people. Many of the original structures have been preserved/renovated as a priceless heritage, now constituting Fayette State Park.*

Probably the most renowned smelters were constructed at Fayette in the Garden Peninsula, where 12,000 acres of choice hardwood timberland were purchased expressly for this purpose. So great was the demand for charcoal that in 1887 and 1888 the company sent woodcutters into forests 15 - 20 miles from the iron works. During peak iron production, nearly 2,500,000 bushels of charcoal were used annually. The wood had to be hauled to the furnaces by wagons over bad roads. Periodic shutdown of the two smelters was dictated by fuel shortages which finally caused an end to Fayette operations in 1890. In its 24 years of operation, Fayette produced 229,000 tons of pig iron.

Noted scholar Harlan Hatcher calculated that during the first half-century of iron production, roughly 330,000 acres of timber were logged for making charcoal; the equivalent of over 500 square miles of forestland.[5] By 1903, when charcoal was being replaced by coke (from bituminous coal)

*Pioneer Charles Paulson carved out a 100-acre homestead in 1884 next to AuTrain Lake in Alger County. The land probably was cleared after the hardwood forest was stripped clean to supply charcoal for the iron smelters at nearby Onota. His cabin was built of hewn white cedar logs, some up to 34 feet long and 22 inches wide on a side. The huge cottonwoods in the yard, native to southern Michigan, are commonly mistaken for a local look-alike cousin, balsam poplar.*

for smelting iron (elsewhere), U.P. blast furnaces were consuming the timber from 10,000 acres of northern hardwoods annually, an average of 30 acres per day. Hatcher remarked that, before we lament, one must remember that at least "this timber was put to good use to convert ore into iron, while in other regions where the stand was equally good it was hewed down, piled up and wastefully burned solely to clear the land for farming."

Any estimate of northern hardwoods acreage cut for industrial purposes must represent a bare minimum of that era's total logging effort. A considerable proportion of the hardwood stands entered into doubtless were not completely razed because of inferior species composition, etc., thereby providing less than the amount of charcoal obtained from better-quality acreage. Additionally, the numerous iron (and copper) miners and woodsworkers cooked and heated their cabins with fuel procured locally. Hardwoods also fueled steam engines used to operate mine hoists, ore crushers, water pumps, and locomotives hauling iron and copper ore to smelters at various locations across the peninsula. One Copper Country historian wrote that "when companies exhausted the closest woodlots, they bought up more distant timber tracts and turned them, too, into acres and acres of stumps." Thus "much of the Keweenaw was clear-cut to feed [the copper industry's] voracious appetite" for wood products. Collectively, therefore, untold thousands of cords of high BTU, pitch-free hardwood were cut and burned each year. After these stands were logged, wildfires frequently raged through the slashings, in what ordinarily was considered an "asbestos forest" with old-growth timber. Once the woody debris was removed (the stumps soon rotted), much of the hardwood acreage was converted to farmland, since the sandy loam soils were considered comparatively well-suited for agriculture. Accordingly, during the latter half of the 1800s, scattered homesteads sprang up like morels after a warm spring rain over much of the central U.P., at least. Furthermore, the Homestead Act of 1862 enabled other settlers to claim 160 acres of unoccupied lands by paying $1.25 an acre, and "improving" the property for five years. Most of these lands were wooded, and had to be cleared before any farming could be done. Eventually, probably several million acres of hardwood forests had been converted to farmlands, many of which were ultimately abandoned because the region's abominable climate was not conducive to profitable agriculture with crop strains then available. (A sage man once observed that "to plow is to pray.") Most abandoned farmland quickly reverted to brush, and eventually became second-growth forests we see today.

# "DAYLIGHT IN THE SWAMP!"

Coincident with, in fact spurred on by, the mining industries was the logging of the region's extensive coniferous swamps. Beginning in the late 1850's, all of the U.P.'s one million acres of white cedar were being systematically clearcut until few if any sizeable virgin stands remained. Surprisingly, there are no detailed records of this logging; hence it almost seems like the work was done surreptitiously. White cedar had a wide variety of uses. (One report told that members of Cartier's expedition up the St. Lawrence River were given a decoction from white cedar fronds called *anneda* by the Indians to cure their scurvy.) Most importantly, it is light and extremely rot-resistant, especially the heartwood. The Indians, and fur traders later on, used split cedar as ribs and planking for birchbark canoes, and covered their wigwams with cedar bark, which they also sold to settlers who needed it to "shingle" their crude log cabins.

In addition to its usefulness in boat and canoe construction, white cedar was cut for small-dimension stakes, fence posts, construction of pole barns, log cabins, for bridge cribbing and stringers, to "corduroy" swamp roads, and as telegraph or telephone poles. Escanaba newspaperman Jean Worth, whose father had been an old-timer "cedar man," reported that cedar logs once were cut into 7-inch lengths for street paving; they worked fine for this purpose, except that a flood could be disastrous! Thousands of carloads of these blocks were shipped by rail; in 1883 alone, 300 carloads were sold at 12 cents per block delivered at Stephenson. Long-lasting white cedar doubtless was the species of choice as timber to shore-up the numerous iron

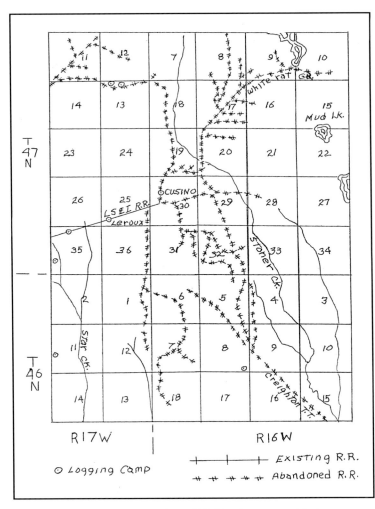

*Extension of the Munising Railway (later LS&I RR) to the townsite of Cusino (Cousineau) at the turn of the century opened up a 40-square mile conifer swamp to logging of its plentiful white cedar then in great demand for various products. The long-abandoned railroad logging grades, outlined as mapped in the mid 1920s, are still visible today as graceful corridors bordered by tall trees. (Michigan Department Conservation; modified.)*

and copper mine tunnels which went as deep as a mile and radiated in all directions from the main shaft following ore drifts. One writer reported that whole forests in the form of "huge sticks" went underground to support the roof or "hanging wall" of Keweenaw copper mines. Another billion board feet was cut into "lags and stulls, or top pieces" used as trusses to prevent mine cave-ins. Iron miners quipped that the best timber was growing underground!

With the advent of rail transportation in the U.P., starting in earnest in the 1880's, countless millions of cedar logs were cut and hewn for railroad ties. On average, a mile of track required over 2,500 eight-foot ties. Thousands of miles of mainlines, logging grades, and spurs were established in an intricate network to move the vast amount of timber being felled for various products from stands scattered throughout the region. Many of these old grades are still visible — indeed, sometimes the original ties can be seen, if dimly — in drier sites. (By comparison, prior to introduction of creosote as a wood preservative, the average life of a jack pine tie north of Lake Superior was about seven years, while tamarack lasted a little longer. No wonder durable cedar ties were so popular.) With rail transportation, the demand for cedar products increased immensely. In 1881 the *Northwestern Lumberman* announced that that year the Chicago market handled 3 million posts, and over 4 million railroad ties headed for the treeless prairie states; which must have involved a significant logging effort.

However, beyond question the single greatest use of white cedar was for shingles. At one time there were 50 shingle mills in the U.P., including one at Shingleton (aptly named) which in 1889 employed 26 men and turned out 6 million shingles a year. Writer Jean Worth told about a ten-block

*This "horse" barn was built long ago, when logging of white cedar began in the adjacent, huge Cusino swamp. Oxen as well as horses probably were housed here, however. Although horses are quicker and stronger, the ruminant oxen proved invaluable in woods work because they could subsist on low quality forage which would soon bring a horse to its knees (as pioneers crossing the Rockies earlier had learned to their sorrow).*

saw invented in Menominee that could use up the wood from a 5-acre cedar swamp in one afternoon. Mill workers were nicknamed shingle-weavers. More often they were called the stub-fingered crew because the saws were hard on a person's digits in those pre-OSHA days. The trade apparently attracted the most reckless men in woods industry employment; roistering, militant, unstable, which earned them the sobriquet of "cedar savages." (The Shingleton bunch reputedly was every bit as tough as the notorious white-piners at Terrible Seney down the road, and numerous grudge fights ensued.)

# RAILROADS IN MICHIGAN
## c. 1910

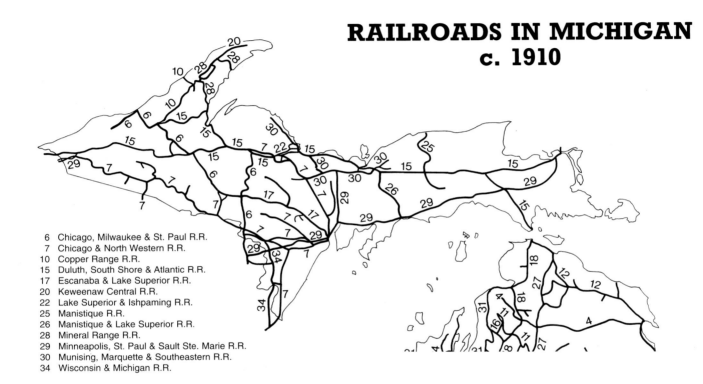

6 Chicago, Milwaukee & St. Paul R.R.
7 Chicago & North Western R.R.
10 Copper Range R.R.
15 Duluth, South Shore & Atlantic R.R.
17 Escanaba & Lake Superior R.R.
20 Keweenaw Central R.R.
22 Lake Superior & Ishpaming R.R.
25 Manistique R.R.
26 Manistique & Lake Superior R.R.
28 Mineral Range R.R.
29 Minneapolis, St. Paul & Sault Ste. Marie R.R.
30 Munising, Marquette & Southeastern R.R.
34 Wisconsin & Michigan R.R.

*Frenzied construction of railroad lines in Upper Michigan got underway in earnest in the 1880s, and soon criss-crossed the region
(some railroads being consolidated and renamed). Train whistles signaled the beginning of the end for the perceived inexhaustible supply of pine
timber, which had all but disappeared by around 1910. (Northern Michigan University Press; modified.)*

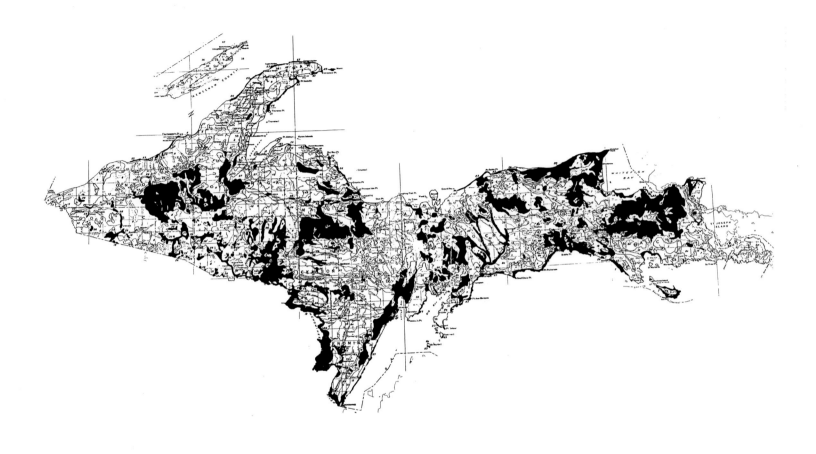

*Based on diagnostic soil characteristics, just 10-15 percent of Upper Michigan's presettlement forests consisted of the celebrated white pine type. More importantly, however, such stands differed widely in relative proportions of white, red, and jack pine, depending upon soil moisture. In many instances the pine types (seven in all) also had a considerable admixture of hardwoods and other conifers, varying in age, species composition, and volume. Well over one-half of the U.P. was stocked in northern hardwoods; approximately one-tenth of the region was covered by conifer swamps, in which white cedar predominated. (Michigan State University; modified.)*

White cedar stands, commonly part of an extensive swamp, usually were logged in winter by small crews in the camp of cedar "jobbers" (but also year round by an individual raising his family nearby). The crews sometimes lived in the same clearing, i.e., landings or townsites, as the sawlog camps run by big lumber companies cutting on adjacent high ground for pine or hardwood. White cedar is very buoyant, thus the cut logs "drove" well on flooded rivers in spring. With the arrival of railroads, little cedar yards popped up almost overnight along their tracks. The logs were hauled by sled to the landings, peeled in spring, and shipped out by rail in summer. The best cedar stands probably were clearcut or high-graded by the turn of the century, although re-entry for residual timber or ingress into formerly inaccessible sites continued for decades afterward. Some of the earliest cutting areas probably were logged again within the next hundred years, where optimum growing conditions prevailed.

# WHEN PINE WAS KING

The first U.P. sawmills to utilize white pine timber, highly prized for its fine-grained, knot-free lumber, were built in Menominee, Delta, and Ontonagon counties between 1832 and 1852. Most of this logging probably was done on a small scale for domestic use, and depended upon a suitable network of rivers to float logs to mills. Advent of railroads sparked the boom in pine logging by permitting ready access into heretofore isolated stands representing the bulk of the type. As an inducement for line extension, the railway companies were granted alternate sections (640 acres) of public land along rights-of-way. Much of this land eventually fell into the hands of "timber barons," who became wealthy tycoons in selling the lumber which built towns and cities as the nation expanded inexorably westward. Logging of the extensive white pine stands began in earnest in much of the U.P. in the 1880s; the onslaught continued unabated for the next 20 years, and finally petered out around 1910, when most sawmills shut down because the supposedly unending supply of timber had been cut. Between 1834 and 1897, the U.P. produced 24.5 billion board feet of pine lumber, a very considerable volume by today's standards. To put it into proper perspective, however, this represented only a small fraction (15 percent) of the total 160.5 billion board feet cut in Michigan over that period. Clearly, the bulk of the pine stumpage grew below the Straits — a fact not widely recognized by U.P. residents.

Volumes have been written about this fascinating era and its flamboyant lumberjacks, and it would be redundant to reiterate here the many bizarre stories and folklore tales that have surfaced since then. Suffice to say that the pine-logging days were highly romanticized. The notion persists that this timber harvest induced the "good-old-days" insofar as game abundance was concerned, but this is a highly erroneous conclusion. To begin with, the pine logging period began well after extensive stands of northern hardwoods were cut for charcoal (or cleared for farmland), and the cedar swamps logged for sundry products. Logging during that earlier time, and over decades to follow, promptly provided very favorable summer and winter range conditions, respectively, for various wildlife, but particularly for the white-tailed deer. For example, initial clearcutting of U.P. swamps *in toto* provided more than enough highly nutritious white cedar browse to have fed the equivalent of one million adult deer over a span of 10 winters! (Or 250,000 deer for 40

*A trainload of giant white pine logs, cut somewhere between Newberry and Seney in 1895, heads for a local sawmill aboard the Duluth, South Shore & Atlantic RR. Between 1834 and 1897, U.P. forests produced 24.5 billion board feet of pine lumber, which amounted to only 15 percent of the 160.5 billion board feet cut during that period state-wide. (Marquette County Historical Society.)*

winters, etc.) The benefits of hardwood logging were a profusion of stump sprouts (coppice regeneration) and seedlings, plus an admixture of highly nutritious succulent forbs and grasses sought after by deer.

In marked contrast, the pine logging primarily involved very large blocks of timber growing on the poorest (sandy) soils in highly localized sites scattered across the U.P. No sane deer would consider spending the winter (100 days or more) in a mature white pine stand before or during logging because it comprises poor habitat in all respects. The repeated wildfires which swept through the slashings after logging only served to exacerbate the problem of inherently low soil fertility for these sites. This scorching not only consumed the thin mantle of organic humus that had accumulated over centuries, but it also effectively sterilized the soil. Consequently, only a few "pioneer" plants (sedges, lichens, shrubs) invaded these sites, and they dominated the ground

*The Lumbermen's Monument on the banks of the Au Sable River near Oscoda provides a somber reminder of the short-lived lusty era when hordes of hardworking lumberjacks went snicker-snack through one magnificent white pine grove after another until nothing remained of the once staggering volume of such timber across Michigan. Sawyers followed on the heels of landlookers (center, likeness of J. M. Longyear, Marquette) who cruised the merchantable stands.*

flora for decades to come. Given this gross lack of food and cover, most game animals shunned these pine barrens except for incidental summer use.

A notable exception to this rule was the ingress of two birds that thrive only in habitats providing open vistas, namely the prairie chicken and sharp-tailed grouse. Once established, these fire-dependent species persevered for many decades before becoming extinct, or existing as mere relics locally in the case of sharptails. Their demise is attributable to a frenetic, almost desperate effort to control wildfires beginning in the 1930s, plus overzealous reforestation programs on these perceived "wastelands;" a practice which persists on public and industrial acreage even today. (The only extensive pine barrens I'm aware of which was not reforested by the 1960s is the 7,000-acre

# FIRE IN THE FOREST

*The fabled Paul Bunyan and Babe, his blue ox (42 ax handles and a plug of tobacco between the horns), have been part of our folklore since the pine-logging days began in the early 1800s in Maine. Paul and Babe live on in our imagination through models such as this, near Ossineke, in Lower Michigan, seeking to attract tourists.*

Kingston Plains in Alger County, where only a last-minute intervention by a concerned professional, who contacted the Governor's office, saved this site from being planted solidly to red pine. I argue, wistfully, that at least a portion of this pine-stump panorama ought to be preserved, i.e., maintained, in its present ethereal state to remind us of the grandeur of the old-growth pine forests before being felled by cross-cut saw and double-bitted ax. The comparatively tiny Hartwick Pines State Park hardly seems a sufficient memorial to this singular by-gone era.)

As alluded to earlier, Upper Michigan's landscape was altered drastically when fires swept through the numerous slashings following logging of the virgin pine. The infamous Peshtigo conflagration roared across 1,280,000 acres of tinder-dry cut-over land in Wisconsin (also crossing into Upper Michigan) in 1871, resulting in a greater loss of human lives (1,200) than in the holocaust striking Chicago that same week. Like most wildfires occurring throughout the Upper Great Lakes during settlement, a carelessly thrown match or lightning bolt would ignite the ubiquitous mounds of resinous fuel with often devastating consequences. Alger County historian Faye Swanberg described one such instance: "For two years around 1900 there was almost no snow or rain.... [In 1902] a fire started near Seney, moved to Grand Marais and on toward Munising, wiping out everything in its path." Since the tract in question takes in a large chunk of real estate, it seems likely that this fire crept along where fuel was scarce, "blowing up" when it reached pine slash and dry marshes, but slowing down where fine fuel was again in short supply; its zig-zag progress was relentless, however, and the searing heat had long-lasting effects on the area. In some places the heat was so intense that the railroad rails were said to have curled into hoops!

Subsequently, grass/litter fires burned the pine barrens repeatedly. Wisconsin biologists noted that they had never found a white pine stump that hadn't been burned black by one or more fires. At first no one expressed much concern for these rampant fires, probably feeling that they helped clear the cut-over land for farms sure to follow. In time,

The stark vista of the huge Kingston Plains in Alger County illustrates the dire consequences of groundfires after the virgin pine was clearcut at around the turn of the century. Burning of the thick slash sterilized the inherently impoverished sandy soil, hence little ecological change has occurred over much of the area since then, as indicated by this 1993 photo. However, plant succession is slowly accelerating as microsite growing conditions improve, owing to natural and planted conifer regeneration which serve as windbreaks and provide shade.

The sentinel white pine in the distance was a mere sapling when the stand was logged a hundred or so years ago. Released from competition, it eventually towered over the red pine seedlings planted by the CCCs in the late 1930s, which now form a dense, tall forest themselves, in what was known as Evelyn Plains, just east of Shingleton. This stately tree had to be felled when M-28 was relocated.

however, the public realized the grave danger and environmental damage posed by these blazes, and sought to suppress them by every means possible. Most such fire-storms were extremely difficult to combat with pick and shovel tools available. Old-timer fire fighters realized the futility of trying to stop a roaring inferno fanned by strong head wind or the air draft produced by towering flames; all they could do was "run like hell and pray for rain."

Gradually the situation changed for the better, until now even a 10-acre grassfire is deemed an unmitigated calamity! The notion still persists, however, that if a fire starts, it potentially could roar across the peninsula literally from Lake Superior to Lake Michigan. This obviously is an alarmist mentality (the Peshtigo Syndrome), since a fire of that magnitude is next to impossible given the current nature of our forests plus modern fire suppression measures. Ironically, the media's sensationalistic reporting of the "Great Seney Fire" in 1976 fostered the perception of inordinate jeopardy associated with wildfires. Although the blaze eventually spread across 35,000 acres, half of it was only lightly burned; much of the remainder was deliberately set on fire in hopes of containing the main blaze. A great deal of this area consisted of dry marshland and fens (string bogs), which in all probability have periodically burned during droughty summers since the last glacier retreated. The purported great loss of "valuable" timber (actually mostly unmerchantable) was grossly

*Artist Alan Asp caught the aesthetic quality of a windswept pine barren by depicting a pair of male sharp-tailed grouse on their dancing ground (lek), where they gather in spring in an effort to entice, hence mate with, discriminating hens. Only small flocks are currently found in remnant openings. Most of their former habitat has been planted to pine, and this bird does not tolerate the lengthening shadows thrown by sapling-sized trees.*

exaggerated; a large share of the damage was attributable to almost fruitless efforts to stop the fire's advance, including a backfire that backfired. The main blaze was declared under control in late summer, with most of the army of fire-fighters being sent home. However, strong south winds and low humidity rekindled the smoldering fire, which leaped across highway M-28. Despite valiant suppression efforts, the fire essentially burned itself out upon reaching the moist, fuelless hardwood ridges miles north of M-28.

The site promptly regenerated with fire-climax species, and it presently is difficult to tell the area had been "scorched," except for occasional charred snags. Many species of wildlife that need semi-open terrain to prosper benefitted greatly from fire-maintenance of such habitat, especially sandhill cranes, woodcock, and black bears. (Despite the food bonanza, deer populations were unaffected because the Seney Refuge lacks suitable winter yarding sites; i.e., they are found there only in summer, and

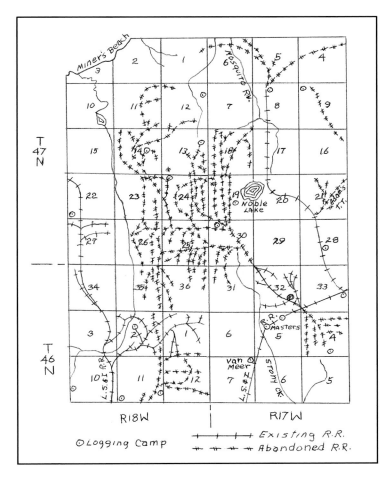

*Pushing the Munising Railway into remote areas enabled the Cleveland-Cliffs Iron Company (CCI) to harvest premium quality hardwood sawlogs from their extensive holdings in Alger County in the early 1900s. Later, many of these sites were strip-logged (i.e., clearcut) to remove the residual "wastewood," cut into 4-foot bolts. CCI shipped untold carloads of this cordwood to its charcoal kilns at Kipling (Delta County) and to chemical distillation plants in Marquette (Cliffs-Dow) via the Munising, Marquette & Southwestern RR (LS&I RR). The systematic network of abandoned logging grades, as mapped in the mid 1920s, are still visible today. (Michigan Department Conservation; modified.)*

*Concerted logging in the U.P. entailed establishment of numerous railroad grades which soon criss-crossed the region. Many sites became sod-bound with grasses and forbs to produce long-lasting openings of great value to game animals and other wildlife. The untreated white cedar ties rotted or were retrieved, leaving innumerable woods-trails accessible by ORVs and 4-WDs to hordes of hunters and fishermen seeking the most secluded places for outings.*

subsequently must leave or perish. Moreover, nearby yards into which deer retreat overwinter now support only small herds because of woefully inadequate food resources.)

Ecologists have long known the profound effects fire has in promoting certain plant (hence animal) communities. Nevertheless, land managers often are reluctant to conduct prescribed burns to achieve desired results (e.g., to produce even-aged stands of jack pine, white cedar, or aspen). Admittedly it takes a certain amount of "intestinal fortitude" to drop a match on heaps of highly flammable slash in fear of producing a blaze which conceivably might rage out of control due to someone's misjudgment, such as an unheeded forecast of a pronounced wind shift.

*While the U.P. was being logged, unscrupulous promoters conned naïve homesteaders into believing that the untilled soils would grow "anything" once the stumps were removed. Several generations probably farmed this acreage until it was abandoned as unprofitable, even though located in "balmy" Menominee County. Most of the buildings were roofed with cedar shingles, the best and cheapest material available during that early era.*

Many birds and mammals that greatly increased in number or immigrated to the U.P. following clearcut and burn of the forests are gradually being squeezed out as their requisite brushy habitat dwindles from natural succession, reduced logging activity, and diligent fire prevention. (An astute colleague was want to say, only partly in jest, "Keep Michigan scrubby—shoot Smokey Bear!") Inevitably, hunters will become increasingly disgruntled that there aren't as many game animals around now compared to their youth; predictably they will blame the situation on perceived ill-advised harvest regulations and/or lack of predator control. Conversely, elitist big-tree buffs will be ecstatic at the wonderful turn of events; and they assuredly will continue to lobby zealously for more "wilderness" areas. (But I for one will miss the spectacular groves of paper birch and lavender fields of fireweed which originate from wildfires. And I will mourn not seeing huge flocks of sharptails soaring out of sight across the pine plains. Regrettably, there already are more than enough red squirrels around to suit me.) And so it goes!

# FROM PAST TO PRESENT

After the initial surge in logging for charcoal production and other fuel needs, new uses for the still extensive northern hardwoods came into being. In 1881, for example, a Wisconsin entrepreneur established a mill across the border in Hermansville to manufacture hardwood flooring from the considerable timber left over after the scattered white pine was high-graded. At peak operation, this firm (IXL, also of Blaney Park fame) owned three railroads, with eight steam engines that hauled timber to its huge yard, which at one point held 30 million board feet of valuable hardwood lumber.

In the late 1890s, hemlock was in great demand in Alger County (and elsewhere) to extract the tannin from its bark for making leather. The bark was brought to East Munising, where a special facility, not surprisingly called The Tannery, was established. By 1905, this plant was turning out 500 hides daily, using 10,000 - 15,000 cords of hemlock bark annually. By the time the company ceased operations in 1920, millions of tons of hemlock bark from the surrounding area had been used in the tanning process. Partly because of the appreciable amount of hemlock timber left in the woods to rot after the bark had been stripped, the Munising Paper Company opened its mill in 1904 to utilize this otherwise wasted cellulose. Soon other mills were built in the U.P. (but more especially in Wisconsin) to manufacture high quality paper and other products from the plentiful supply of long-fibered conifer pulpwood.

There was a resurgence of logging activity during both WWI and WWII. The demand for attractive veneers, notably birdseye and curlymaple, steadily increased, as did the use of hardwood lumber for fine furniture. Recently the market for dense-fibered hardwood pulp has substantially improved. Yet, on a peninsula-wide basis, the U.P. forests are growing twice as much wood (raw cellulose) than is currently being harvested; namely, 3.8 million vs. 1.7 million cords, respectively. This striking imbalance between the annual allowable cut (net wood increment) and timber removal is difficult for laymen to visualize. Suffice to say that the average diameter of sawlogs brought to the mills has steadily declined under intensive forest management, thus shorter and shorter rotations.

*Shortly after turn of the century, ambitious attempts were made to farm open marshes underlaid with organic soils by using steam draglines to dredge long ditches so as to drain the land. Numerous main and collateral ditches were dug in Schoolcraft County to establish the Bullock Ranch (Holland Ditch, photo) and Mint Farm (Big Ditch), for example, which turned out to be expensive, abortive endeavors. Many of these areas are the last stronghold of species like the sandhill cranes, which require open habitat to prosper.*

*Vast shallow marshes intersected by narrow islands or sand strips were converted into waterfowl habitat in the mid-1930s by constructing dikes to form a series of large pools whose water level could be regulated by spillways to promote aquatic plants. The resultant Seney National Wildlife Refuge in Schoolcraft County provides needed habitat for a multitude of aquatic plants and animals. The initial goal of producing a Canada goose "factory" was not achieved because of a malaria-like disease (Leucocytozoon) transmitted by blackflies that kills the bulk of goslings hatched in bad years. Additionally, unless controlled, predation on goslings by northern pike, snapping turtles, and raccoons (eggs) can be considerable. Currently the Refuge is being used to reestablish a nesting flock of trumpeter swans in Michigan.*

When I came to Shingleton in 1953, a grizzled pulpcutter told me that as a lad he had stood atop Buck Hill, a promontory near the hamlet of Melstrand, and was able to see Lake Superior, a few miles northward, as well as Lake Michigan nearly 40 miles to the south! A tongue-in-cheek story to be sure, although not absolutely outlandish. For unquestionably, in little more than half a century, most of the virgin timber had been razed and the sites scorched by wildfires or cleared for farming until almost no tall trees remained. The devastation was so great that much of the U.P. became the "land nobody wanted," and the poorest acreage reverted to state ownership for non-payment of property taxes. Essentially the same clearcut and burn situation prevailed throughout the Great Lakes region.[6]

*Groves of paper birch promptly become established following clearcutting or burning, and persist as even-aged trees until replaced by shade-tolerant (climax) species.  Few vistas are so aesthetically pleasing, especially during peak autumn color.*

Most of Upper Michigan's forests, especially its hardwood stands, today range from approximately 65 - 130 years old. The once extensive tracts of aspen (formerly considered a "weed-tree," but now an important pulpwood), resulting from earlier site conversion, are gradually reverting to northern hardwoods, the climax type on better soils, except where this "popple" is being regenerated by clearcutting.[7] Aside from special instances (e.g., liquidation harvest), all-aged regimes for northern hardwoods through selection logging does not disturb the ground sufficiently to foster fruiting plants and forage of value to game. Beech, a very desirable mast producer, often is marked for cutting (along with hemlock) just to eliminate it from a stand because its wood is worth less at the mill than that of associate species. Consequently, the current discriminatory trend, whether inadvertent or deliberate, is toward creation of monotypic stands of sugar maple — a practice which does not represent sound forest management.

*Fields of fireweed signify site disturbance, typically from a ground, or litter, fire. Once established, these attractive lavender "weeds" persist for decades, eventually being shaded-out by inexorably encroaching woody plants.*

Moreover, many pole-size northern hardwoods are so densely stocked as to limit their usefulness for wildlife unless small clearings are made in these stands expressly to boost their carrying capacity for desired animals. Proper diversity of the forest is the key to good game (and timber) management.

Present-day white cedar stands generally are less than 135 years old, having become established following the initial surge in logging, although trees twice that age or more, representing the residual stems where old-growth timber was high-graded, may also be present. Many originally pure cedar stands converted to less desirable mixed conifers or conifer/hardwoods following "choppers'-choice" logging, especially if the accompanying slash did not burn after cutting. Because pole-size white cedar provides good thermal shelter for deer in winter, the Michigan DNR has declared a virtual moratorium on further logging of state-owned swamps, whereas, conversely, such vital "green barns" are being indiscriminately leveled

*Trained personnel not only bring wild fires quickly under control, but they now also conduct burns prescribed for regenerating fire-climax forest types, as shown here igniting slash from a clearcut white cedar swamp. If well planned and conducted, such fires pose little risk of jumping set boundaries. Yet an inordinate (but unwarranted) fear that devastating fires can occur today still persists in the public's mind.*

elsewhere. The future welfare of white-tailed deer requires that these deeryards be intensively managed according to prescribed practices to perpetuate their cyclic production of forage. If left as is (i.e. "saved"), cedar yards will steadily deteriorate in protective value for wintering deer with advancing stand age until they can no longer survive there. Sadly, most forest managers lack the technical sophistication and strong motivation to formulate long-range plans for swamp conifer deeryard rehabilitation. Heavy harvest of hemlock in "river-bottom yards" in the western U.P. has all but eliminated deer in these areas because highly effective canopy cover is now absent or in short supply. It will require numerous groves of century-old hemlocks in the right places to reverse that population trend.

*A spring broadcast burn on a clearcut swamp conifer site was immediately followed by dense seeding-in of pioneering ground flora, plus germination of seeds buried under the mantle of organic debris. Mother Nature soon camouflaged what initially was a hideous fire scar; the price of forest renewal.*

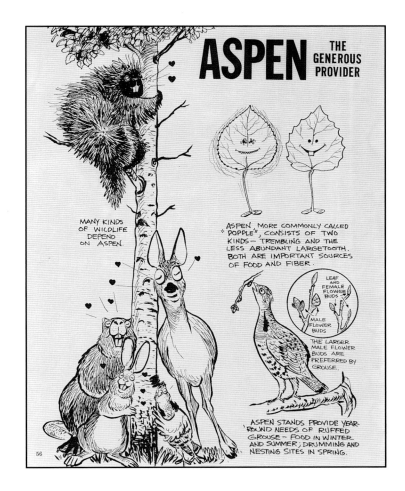

Michigan biologist/illustrator Oscar (Ozz) Warbach masterfully depicts the importance of aspen for wildlife, as well as for man. This forest type can be perpetuated only by clearcutting or burning, so as to produce even-aged trees growing in full sunlight. Hence, without such treatment, "popple" stands soon revert to long-lasting conifer/hardwood types of lesser value to game animals. (Michigan Department Natural Resources.)

*The sporting appeal of deer hunting is exemplified by the sight of a startled buck in mid-leap while fleeing from imminent danger detected via extremely acute senses. Adrenalin levels peak sharply in prey and would-be predators alike in such brief encounters during the hunting season. Deer hunting is a consuming passion for most U.P. men (and some Dianas).*

# 6

## THE CERVIDS

### WHITE-TAILED DEER

Although it is impossible to estimate with any certainty the population density of white-tailed deer in Upper Michigan during presettlement time, the consensus is that region-wide their numbers were very low. Wisconsin biologists surmised that prior to 1800 the hardwood/conifer forests in that state on average supported less than 10 deer per square mile. Early accounts pertaining to deer numbers in the colonies and midwest frontier often noted extreme differences in their abundance locally. On the surface, such wide discrepancies are hard to reconcile. As one example, the leader of a French military campaign against the Fox Indians in the Green Bay area in 1728 reported: "Our savages went into the woods, but soon returned bringing with them several roebucks. This species of game is very common at this place, and we were enabled to lay in several days' provisions of it." This was enough venison to feed 400 soldiers plus their 1,000 Indian allies. Since this locale borders the northern forest biome, unusually favorable habitats must have prevailed to foster such high densities of deer, perhaps as a result of a natural (or incendiary) forest fire.

Biologists now believe that whitetails evolved under range conditions that provided irregular food cycles of feast or famine. Over eons they developed physiologic and sociologic means of maximizing their welfare during ideal stages, while minimizing adversity during hard times sure to follow. The up-and-down fluctuation in forage resources ordinarily occurred fortuitously and in a patchy distribution; a windstorm or burn soon resulted in a nutritional cornucopia, which peaked and then dwindled to a point of food scarcity. The question is: how did deer manage to cope with such unstable, unpredictable forage conditions?

The basic social unit in deer is the family group, consisting of a matriarch doe, several generations of daughters, and their collective fawns. The matriarch is very dominant and assertive; she selects the better food for herself and defends the best parturition site against daughters or subordinate neighbors. Experience has made the matriarch extremely wary, hence family members follow her lead in avoiding predation and other potential disasters. With adequate nutrition, a doe's reproductive success reaches its inherent maximum. Physically prime mothers exhibit high fecundity, usually conceiving twins but occasionally triplets or quadruplets. Their fawns are born large and healthy, and grow rapidly because of abundant milk. Even yearling does may produce twins. Under superb diet (plus lack

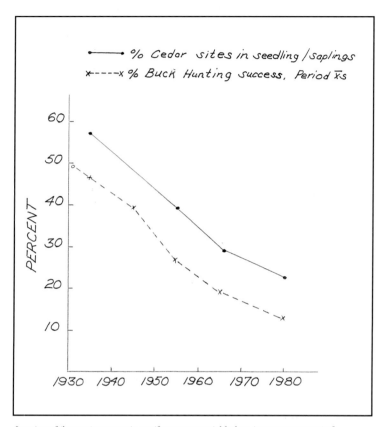

% Cedar sites in seedling/saplings
% Buck Hunting success, Period x̄s

Logging of the vast acreage in conifer swamps yielded an immense amount of nutritious white cedar browse from the resultant even-aged sapling regeneration. Deer herds literally ate their way through such stands as the population soared. Eventually, however, deer browsed all the reachable forage, and their welfare suffered. Changes in the proportion of total white cedar acreage consisting of seedling/sapling stands for the periods surveyed correlated closely with mean annual percentage of successful buck hunters in Upper Michigan over the years indicated.

of maternal domination), 50 percent or more of the doe fawns reach puberty, conceiving a singleton or sometimes twins when bred. Prime-age does typically give birth to a disproportionate number of female progeny; birth of daughters

almost assures a mother that she can achieve (or maintain) hierarchical status — a very strong drive. Conversely, yearlings and (especially) precocious doe fawns ordinarily produce more male offspring. These young mothers have little chance of forming their own family group; thus their best choice is to produce a son who will emigrate elsewhere, hopefully to good new range, and become an alpha (dominant) buck. This will optimize his reproductive ability, thereby passing on his mother's genes to numerous grandchildren. A surplus of female births coincident with high fecundity during plentiful food results in a herd increasing at an almost exponential rate.

In contrast, a mature doe in relatively poor vigor during the rut, as when she hasn't fully recovered from the considerable nutritional drain of pregnancy and lactation, is more apt to conceive a singleton, quite likely a male. Sub-par vitality in a yearling doe causes infertility or low fecundity because survival and growth take precedence over reproduction. Moreover, very few (if any) doe fawns become sexually mature under limited rations, when their growth is seriously stunted. Severe famine during pregnancy will expedite a population's decline from resultant high neonatal mortality. Virtually all of the season's fawn crop may be lost because there are too many stillbirths, the fawns are runts and are too weak to stand and nurse, the mother has no milk, or she lacks maternal instinct and abandons her offspring.

The fact that progeny sex ratios in deer (and other animals) can vary significantly from the theoretical 50:50 is a new and exciting concept which warrants discussion. In low populations, when deer are widely scattered, or if bucks are in short supply due to hunting harvest, a doe in estrus

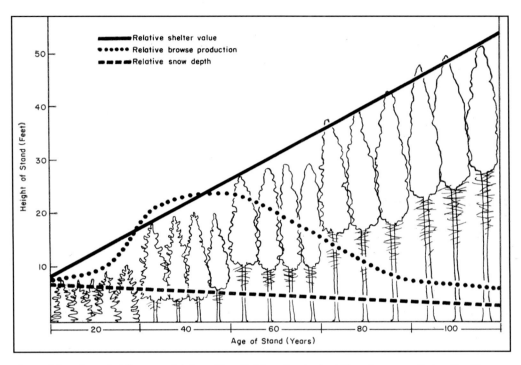

*Research has shown that the sequential clearcutting of white cedar stands yields optimum quantity/quality of browse or shelter at different stages in the rotation cycles of even-aged stands so produced. Unfortunately, most cedar yards are currently stocked in century-old trees of great shelter value, but which provide scant nutritious browse for wintering deer. (Journal Forestry.)*

may not be able to find a mate until late in her 24-hour period of receptivity. (When he doesn't find her, she will seek him out by walking miles if necessary to mark, i.e., urinate on, the "scrapes" he made to advertize his availability as stud.) Breeding toward the close of her cycle typically results in a disproportionate conception of males, compared to more females when insemination occurs early in estrus because sires are numerous. The mechanism by which nature tries to balance the sexes is complex and still in need of elucidation.

Simply stated, the outcome hinges largely on the differential motility/viability of the X versus Y spermatozoa, which yields a female or a male, respectively, in fertilizing an X ovum. The odds that a doe will produce either sons or daughters varies according to a host of biologic (e.g., age and nutrition) and sociologic (e.g., isolation or crowding) factors.

Because of such reproductive characteristics, the ability of deer to promptly fill a newly-created niche of prime habitat

*By midwinter, Upper Michigan deer ordinarily are belly-deep in snow when searching for browse away from hard-packed runways they maintain under a dense conifer canopy. Such foraging is energetically exhausting, and exposes deer to severe air chill and increased risk of predation; all of which can be hazardous to their health. (Michigan Department Natural Resources.)*

is nothing short of phenomenal. Fortunately, the same self-population control mechanisms serve as a brake to keep deer from overwhelming their range. The remarkable thing is not that herds sometimes overshoot the habitat's carrying capacity (rarely static), but that this happens so seldom, even in the absence of natural predators (except inept humans).

Although whitetails are not "northern" mammals in a strict sense, they nevertheless evolved in regions of comparatively rigorous winters. Their first line of defense against climatic adversity is to accumulate large quantities of visceral and subcutaneous fat. Lipogenesis is an obligatory physiological process that occurs in autumn even despite acute food deprivation because ample body fat (obesity) is crucial to overwinter survival. Thus fat production takes precedence over growth or estrual activity. (Lipogenesis is triggered by declining levels of prolactin, a pituitary hormone, tuned to decreasing daylength, or photoperiod, which changes most rapidly at the autumnal equinox.)

In midwinter, when nutritious forage is hard to come by, even well-fed deer voluntarily reduce food intake and adopt a torpid, or semi-hibernating, state in an inherent (primordial) effort to conserve vital energy. They then spend much of their time loafing or bedded under a tight conifer canopy to minimize body heat loss via thermal radiation and convection. In northern climes deer congregate, or "yard," in lowland sites providing good physical comfort (but conversely scant browse) beneath the dense, self-pruned overstory. They restrict travel to a network of hard-packed snow trails as a further means of conserving energy (as well as to better evade predators). Stored fat is slowly catabolized for energy to maintain body functions in the face of grave food deficiency. If the winter is excessively prolonged and harsh, lipid reserves ultimately are exhausted, and muscle break-down begins, at which point the innate defense mechanisms collapse and the animal dies. "Starved" deer exhibit a paunch full of poor-quality browse which could not be digested by rumen microflora to supply energy. It is well to reiterate, however, that surprisingly few deer (except for small fawns) succumb to winter attrition unless horrendously bad conditions prevail. A late-winter blizzard can be particularly devastating because by then they have "shifted gears" upward to normal physiological levels, hence the body no longer is resilient to stress. A weather severity index derived from the cumulative ratings for air chill and snow hazard (depth plus its supporting ability) serves to monitor such dire prospects for Michigan deer over a 20-week winter season.

European settlement in the Upper Great Lakes eventually resulted in a mosaic of clearings yielding abundant ground flora, shrubs, and small trees which provided diverse and nutritious forage for deer. Winter logging furnished ample browse from felled tops, especially unexcelled white cedar, within easy reach. Deer responded quickly, extending their range northward almost to Hudson Bay. The herd on either side of the Mackinac Straits probably reached its initial peak between 1875 and 1886. During this period more than 100,000 deer were killed by market-hunters and shipped via railroads to customers in populated areas southward. In March 1873, The (Marquette) Mining Journal reported that four men killed 158 deer to supply meat for lumber camps in the Whitefish River vicinity (probably cedar cutters). Market-hunters were greed personified. A newspaper story dated October 1885, told that 17,500 pounds of venison were shipped by rail from Munising to Detroit, whereas another line shipped 18,000 pounds of "saddles" (i.e., only the loins and hams — the rest of a carcass probably being left for furred and feathered scavengers). That same month 700 dressed deer carcasses were shipped by rail from nearby AuTrain. Because of excessive market-hunting, herd densities plummeted. In 1895, therefore, the Michigan legislature felt obliged to shorten the hunting season, restricting it to the 1st through 15th of November, and limited each sportsman to 5 deer per season. Even so, the first year 14,477 licenses were sold at fifty cents apiece. Commercial hunting for out-of-state markets was not strictly enforced until 1900, when it became a federal offense (Lacy Act) to transport illegally-taken game animals across state lines.

With market-hunting banned, effective anti-poaching efforts, bucks-only hunting regulations, and lush year round habitat, the U.P. deer herd rebounded to its all-time high in the 1930s, 40s, and 50s. Soon the range was overstocked, and serious starvation losses occurred in severe winters. This culminated in the bombastic "deer-wars" fought between Michigan sportsmen, egged-on by the media and politicians, and DNR biologists as to what constituted sound herd management, namely bucks-only or any-deer harvest. The bitterness that ensued still endures 50 years after it all began. The begrudging acceptance of antlerless deer hunting predictably will be challenged as soon as herd numbers decline significantly following back-to-back hard winters. Since those heydays, the population trend has been inexorably downward, except in areas of continued heavy logging activity and expanding agriculture, which collectively provide good nutrition. In other areas the forest is rapidly maturing, thus becoming of marginal value for deer. Owing to a succession of unusually easy yarding seasons,

however, modest population increases have materialized in certain areas within the past decade. (In view of these atypically mild winters, maybe the sky **is** falling down, as some climatologists assert!)

Celebrated photographer/naturalist George Shiras III reported that in 1870 deer were rarely seen on the north shore of Lake Superior, where they later became numerous, and few were found along the south shore close to the lake because Ojibway Indians camped and hunted near stream mouths during summer. Shiras went on to say that prior to the late 1800's,

> "On the south shore of Lake Superior,including all northern Michigan and Wisconsin, there once existed a spring and fall movement of white-tailed deer that possessed all the characteristics of a true migration.... Early in May as soon as the depth of snow permitted travel, thousands of deer worked their way north from their wintering ground near Lake Michigan or into Wisconsin, traveling alone into a broad belt a little back from the south shore of Lake Superior, where a few weeks later the fawns were born. The bucks came more leisurely, but by early May the migration was over."

Furthermore, according to Shiras,

> "Sometimes as early as August 15, on the coming of the first north winds and light frost, the does, fawns, and yearlings started south and by September thousands were on their

*way, regardless of the fact that no snow would fall for another six weeks, and none deep enough to interfere with the food supply or freedom of movement for more than three months."*

The fall migration was ascribed to deep snow along the Lake Superior coast, which the animals sought to avoid:

> *"Deer traveled southward on many trails, which by centuries of use had become about two feet broad, clear of obstructions, and deeply cut in banks and soft ground. In swamps they were like the caribou trails found in Newfoundland."*

Shiras said the migrations ended with the building of wire fences along railroads, which prevented free movement of deer and forced them into winter yards where they fell prey to wolves and lawless hunters:

> *"Thus ended the deer migrations. Today all the great runways are obliterated by bushes and fallen trees. Contrary to expectations, the deer soon adjusted themselves to their permanent home near the south shore of the lake."* (Snow or no snow!)

This fascinating account unfortunately is a myth and ought not to be cited as gospel. Shiras was too young to have witnessed these migrations himself, but instead must have relied on the recollections of older settlers and Indians for his information. To begin with, fawning period in the U.P. begins — not ends —in late May. Deer movements toward winter yards start only after bitter cold weather or a blizzard forces them to seek respite in dense coniferous cover; such weather seldom exists until mid-November or early December. Tagging studies have shown that some Wisconsin deer traditionally yard in the U.P., as well as vice versa. Maximum seasonal movements rarely exceed 30 miles, let alone hundreds of miles as implied by Shiras. Anyone familiar with whitetails knows they can easily bound over a 6 or 7 foot barrier, and wouldn't let a mere barbed-wire fence deter them. In contradiction, Shiras stated: "It is well known that deer will not jump even a low obstruction placed in the general direction they are traveling." (But he also said that whitetails are solitary creatures and "seldom associate with others of [their] kind" — which we've come to know is untrue.) Shiras was correct in comparing the centuries-old, deeply-cut trails in question to those made by caribou in Newfoundland; in all probability he was actually reporting the migratory behavior manifested by woodland caribou that formerly resided in the U.P. These animals were on the verge of extinction by the time deer became numerous in U.P. areas he later became familiar with.

The most convincing reason for believing that Michigan's deer population historically was low is that other cervids — moose, caribou, elk — were once fairly common across most of the state. It is now known that whitetails harbor an internal parasite with the imposing scientific name of *Parelaphostrongylus tenuis*, alias "brain worm." Deer having this parasite pass innumerable microscopic first-stage larva in their feces (pellets), which eventually penetrate the footpad of their intermediate host, certain species of terrestrial snails or slugs. The latter become encysted on vegetation, and the infective stage of the parasite is ingested when the definitive host eats the forage. The larva bore through the rumen wall and migrate to the meninges of the brain (hence it is also called meningeal worm), where they become adults, mate, and lay eggs, thus completing their life cycle.

Deer evidently contracted this parasite early in their evolution and developed an immunity to it during long symbiotic association. In other cervids, however, the larva cause extensive tissue damage to the animal's spinal cord in their journey to the brain. This trauma results in characteristic symptoms including unusual docility, muscular weakness, blindness, and other neurologic disorders, which frequently culminate in the animal's death. (Earlier, some biologists thought that such "moose disease" possibly was caused by a deficiency of soil cobalt, an element required by ruminants for vitamin $B_{12}$ production.) It now is clear that whitetails evolved separately, i.e., in different biomes or ecosystems, from those frequented by other cervids because the latter have little or no immunity to *P. tenuis* infections. In essence, deer devised a highly effective (albeit insidious) means of eliminating direct food competition from allied ruminants. We don't know the density of deer needed to kill off sympatric cervids, because it probably "all depends." Under the conditions of primeval Michigan, perhaps just a few deer concentrated in a forage-rich patch were enough to contaminate the site with brain worm, thereby getting rid of other antlered species or at least severely restricting their trespass, thus minimizing food competition.

# MOOSE

Moose have been present in Michigan since early post-glacial times, and were an important source of food and clothing for the prehistoric people. The highest moose populations in Michigan prior to European settlement probably existed in the U.P., where the transition-zone habitat was more favorable than downstate. One report in the Jesuit Relations said that in 1661 at L'Anse, during spring "the savages are living on moose meat which comes [sic] very opportunistically." Father Gabriel Dreuillettes, stationed at Sault Ste. Marie in 1671, related that after miraculously regaining his sight in church, an aged Indian returned to the woods to set his moose traps (probably snares) all winter long.

Moose were a large and tempting target for U.P. settlers and miners, and by 1889 their numbers had been reduced so low that the Michigan Legislature granted the animals complete legal protection, a law still in effect. Even without hunting, however, the moose would have fallen victim to the paralyzing effects of brain worm infection spread by the burgeoning deer herd. Moose fared much better on Isle Royale, which they had occupied since early times — and where deer never existed. Between 1870 and 1900, extensive logging of the boreal forest, followed by wildfires, produced great quantities of forage for Isle Royale moose, which increased from an estimated 200 in 1916 to well over 2,000 in 1926. By then they had seriously overexploited the range, resulting in incipient (and prospectively heavy) starvation mortality. Four possible avenues were considered by the Michigan Conservation Commission to rectify the problem of severe range damage on Isle Royale:

*Unlike the endeavor 50 years earlier when Isle Royale moose were caught in wooden boxtraps and brought by ship to the U. P., recent restocking efforts employed state-of-the-art technology featuring a potent immobilizing drug injected via a dart-gun fired from a hovering helicopter at animals crossing frozen lakes. Sedated animals were air-lifted to a handling site, placed into special crates, and trucked from Algonquin Provincial Park, Ontario, overnight for release on the Peshekee Grade north of Michigamme during the 1985 and 1987 winters. (Michigan Department Natural Resources.)*

artificially feed the moose; reduce the herd by introducing their natural predator, the wolf (coyotes were already there); allow moose hunting by sportsmen or state-paid hunters; or livetrap excess moose for release in the U.P. In their wisdom the Commissioners considered the moose trapping program to be the least of these evils; in retrospect this was a bad choice because it was ineffectual as well as very expensive.

During the winters of 1934-35, 1935-36, and 1936-37, 71 moose (representing less than 5 percent of the herd!) were captured on Isle Royale and transported by boat to the mainland. Of these, 18 were released in the Keweenaw Peninsula, 17 in the Escanaba River Tract (Marquette County), and 34 brought to the Cusino Game Refuge (Schoolcraft County). Two moose were given to the Detroit Zoological Park, and six were kept at the newly-established Cusino Wildlife Experiment Station for special studies. Six calves, some of them conceived on Isle Royale, were born in captivity; two of them died within a few days of birth despite bottle feeding. The experimental animals were disposed of after WWII began, when the study had to be terminated.

Moose sightings or tracks were frequently reported following the main releases, but, according to biologists, such records gradually declined until "the population [was] only a remnant." The prevailing sentiment was that the released moose were being maliciously killed by "disgruntled hunters;" a seemingly logical but inaccurate deduction (though some animals surely were poached by hungry cedar-savages — incorrigible violators). The 1965-66 Biennial Report noted that 25 - 50 moose was a reasonable estimate of actual numbers in the U.P. Many, if not most, of these animals were thought to have emigrated from Ontario either by swimming the St. Marys River or crossing it on the ice (and over Whitefish Bay.)

As white-tailed deer continued to decline in the deep snow belt along Lake Superior from winter malnutrition, interest in restocking the U.P. with moose increased within the DNR's Wildlife Division. Nonetheless, the 1975-76 Biennial Report noted that "Investigations into the potential of Michigan's Upper Peninsula as moose range led to the conclusion that prospects for producing a huntable population were virtually nil, and that the cost-benefit ratio of an introduction was unfavorable." This pronouncement was duly ignored. The rationale which ensued was that the area north of Michigamme might be able to support 500 moose, with an additional 300 in the Seney area and 100 more in the Keweenaw. Accordingly, in 1985 and 1987, 60 moose were captured in midwinter in Ontario's Algonquin Provincial Park and liberated near the Peshekee Grade north of Michigamme.

The transplanted moose are reproducing at an unknown rate. Current herd size is difficult to ascertain with any precision, but one authority sets the 1994 "count" at 265 animals; not a high overall increment. The release site apparently is not yet overbrowsed, thus most calves should be born healthy. Black bears constitute a serious predator on moose calves, especially twinnings, since the mother cannot (or will not) defend both young simultaneously, as their beds are widely spaced for such contingencies. (Moose calves can hardly outrun a hungry bear; one was known to kill a 27-day-old fawn, a remarkable feat because even at that young age fawns are extremely agile, swift runners.) The bear population probably is robust within the remote rugged release area.

Wolves are the only other potential predator on moose calves. Illegal killing of moose (wanton shooting, poaching, "mistaken identity" by deer hunters) will affect herd dynamics, as in past years. The greatest danger, or limiting factor, however, is posed by brainworm infections. Numerous deaths attributable to this parasite have been verified by necropsy on fresh carcasses found in and around the release site thus far. The incidence of such mortality could climb markedly if the deer herd continues to increase because of mild winters and/or expanded logging effort locally. Greater occurrence of *P. tenuis* infection might stabilize the moose herd at relatively low density, precluding even a token hunting season, as biologists initially hoped for.

# WOODLAND CARIBOU

The woodland subspecies of caribou (vs. barren-ground or tundra animals) evidently was never abundant in Michigan or Wisconsin. However, it exhibited the same distribution in Michigan as the moose, even being recorded in the extreme southeast portion of the state. Caribou were also found as late as the 1850s on Beaver Island, but were considered to visit the area only rarely, when ice covered Lake Michigan. The 1921-22 Biennial Report stated that the 225 - 300 caribou on Isle Royale in 1920 may have represented a migrating herd which returned north on the ice to Ontario; the last record of caribou on that island was in 1926. Indians were reported feasting on caribou at Carp Lake in Chippewa County in March 1849. Records for Upper Michigan indicate that the species was found here as late as 1910, if not till 1912. The purported "deer

*Artist Charles Schafer sketched the then-extirpated Michigan mammals in a 1950 publication. The marten and fisher have since been reintroduced, the lynx remains a rare itinerant visitor, the wolverine and woodland caribou probably will never be returned here, whereas the mountain lion is deemed the "phantom cat" in the U.P. There doesn't appear to be much public clamor to restock the prairie of southwestern Michigan with bison, where they once used to roam before being eaten by sod-buster settlers. (Michigan Department Conservation.)*

migration" described by George Shiras quite likely consisted of caribou that shifted from the U.P. to spend winters in Wisconsin. Shiras noted, however, that the only instance he knew of caribou on the south shore of Lake Superior was an account given him by his old Indian guide, of a small band of about half a dozen, all of which the guide shot about 12 miles southeast of Marquette in 1865. Caribou may have been especially vulnerable to hunting by Indians (and to wolf predation) during their wanderings to and from northern Wisconsin.

Unlike deer and moose, woodland caribou respond negatively to logging and burning of the forest, at least in the short term. They thrive best in a boreal (coniferous) environment intermingled with northern hardwoods, white cedar swamps, black spruce bogs, and scattered openings. Their staple diet in winter consists of ground lichens (reindeer "moss") augmented by arboreal lichens (old-man's-beard) when available. Since caribou must paw away snow ("cratering") with their oversize hooves to feed, migrating away from the deep-snow belt along Lake Superior would have constituted an effective adaptation from a bioenergetics standpoint. During the snow-free season, caribou consume various herbaceous, shrubby, and aquatic plants. Any habitat change which eliminates their preferred food is detrimental to this specialized ruminant.

Wolves, lynx, and bears are major predators on woodland caribou. The species exists in modest numbers on the Slate Islands of Ontario and northern environs bordering Lake Superior only because wolves and lynx are absent here (these predators prefer to hunt moose and snowshoe hares inland). The rugged shoreline habitat allows caribou to escape wolves, and the offshore islands provide safe calving sites. Lynx are serious predators on caribou calves in Newfoundland, if not wherever they coexist; bobcats probably can be included in that context. Newborn caribou are "followers," so called because they are precocious and can amble along at mother's heel soon after birth, when the cows must band together in moving to safety. (In contrast, whitetail fawns are "hiders," evading predation by lying still for long periods and blending into the background of a bed via their cryptic coloration, i.e., concealing spotted coat. The statement that fawns have no body odor has not been substantiated, and probably is a fallacy; this is not to be confused with development of their scent glands.)

Caribou were released (reintroduced?) on Grand Island by the private landowners in 1916 for aesthetic purposes, but they failed to survive. The first group reportedly plunged to their death over a high cliff while being pursued by a pack of wolves. The second group evidently suffered badly from ectoparasites (warble fly larva, or bots?) and soon perished. In 1922, Michigan imported 60 reindeer (domesticated Old World caribou) from Norway. The 10 bulls and 50 cows were temporarily penned in Ingham county, where they dropped 12 calves. They were then shipped to Grayling and released in a fenced corral, but finally were rounded up and placed in a four-square mile enclosure (where reindeer moss was plentiful) north of Newberry, in Luce County. Within two years only seven of the original animals were still alive, and many calves had been lost. In 1927, the lone survivor, an old cow, was sent to the Belle Isle Zoo in Detroit. In retrospect this stocking attempt was doomed to failure because of almost certain deer brain worm infections. In all fairness, however, the presence (and lethal impact) of that parasite was then still unknown. Any attempt to reintroduce woodland caribou into the U.P. (as tried various times elsewhere) in all probability will prove unsuccessful because of *P. tenuis;* additionally, spring and summer ranges must provide adequate escape cover against prospective predators. Whether current U.P. habitat is indeed suitable for caribou, and whether they can survive in the deep snow belt without being "trained" to migrate south, is problematic.

# ELK

Elk, the fourth member of Cervidae in the New World, are now considered by taxonomists to be the same species as the Old World red deer. Its preferred common name is wapiti, derived from the Cree word "wapitik" for white deer, or from a Shawnee word meaning white rump. In prehistoric times elk ranged as far north as southern Quebec, and in some places as far east as the Atlantic coast. There is solid evidence that elk occurred in most if not all counties in Lower Michigan but were extirpated by 1877. Yellowstone elk (a different subspecies) were released in the Pigeon River area between 1915 and 1919; their descendants are now legally hunted, under tight regulations, mainly to reduce farm crop/forest tree damage. Elk probably were present in some parts of the U.P. in small numbers since ancient times, although this has not been firmly documented. The possible bones of elk were unearthed from an archeological dig in Delta County.

Moreover, as there is definite proof that elk were present in Iron and Vilas Counties across the border in Wisconsin, it seems quite reasonable that they also were found in that vicinity in the U.P. Elk prefer clearings to dense forests; thus most of our region may not have been to their liking.

The Indians assuredly hunted elk wherever they were found. The same carnivores that prey upon moose and caribou also chase elk. Elk are highly adaptable browsers and grazers (generalist feeders) and have a prodigious, catholic appetite. A western biologist likened the animal to a king-sized vacuum cleaner! Hence they are (or would become) serious competitors with deer and moose for food. Elk are highly social animals and need more solitude than deer, which readily adjust to, or tolerate, human disturbance. Elk likewise are susceptible to the ravages of brain worm, and do not thrive where deer are numerous. (A colleague wildlife pathologist hypothesized that the uncommonly tame behavior of Pigeon River elk afflicted with this sickness made them particularly vulnerable to poaching, or wanton killing, by local malefactors; a quite reasonable inference.)

A dozen elk were released on Grand Island around the turn of the century and soon increased to an estimated 250 animals. Under supplemental feeding and protection from wolves (and hunters), the herd of whitetails, including a large number of albinos, also increased to roughly 3,000, or 150 per square mile — an exceedingly high density. After its initial success, the elk herd perished from range overbrowsing on the limited area (20 square miles) stocked mainly in mature northern hardwoods. The deer likewise dwindled to a remnant herd until Grand Island was heavily logged, beginning in the late 1950s. Brain worm doubtless also contributed to the elk herd's demise, however, as in the caribou restocking incident.

# 7

# WILD CANIDS

## WOLF

The gray (alias timber) wolf was found in all counties of Michigan when the white man arrived. Their numbers probably were relatively low because they had to subsist mainly on moose and caribou, which likewise were present in low abundance. Moreover, healthy moose in particular are hard for wolves to bring down. Mammalogist Hartley Jackson estimated (probably overoptimistically) that in the early 1800s there may have been twenty to twenty-five thousand wolves in Wisconsin. Wolf populations increased greatly as deer, their favorite prey, increased astronomically following settlement of the region. Probably many thousand wolves roamed throughout Michigan at their peak in the latter half of the 1800s, despite being extensively hunted and trapped for bounties paid by state and local governments. Ontario biologists remarked that during the period of deer abundance in Algonquin Provincial Park, wolves were persecuted relentlessly, but they were never commoner at any time in known history. As the forests continued to mature following earlier logging, deer could not gain as much food energy as they physically expended in searching for it in deep snow, and their population plunged. Although wolves are no longer hounded by man, they have become less abundant since their prey-base fell below a critical threshold. These researchers concluded that "One can hardly blame the [current] shortage of deer in Algonquin Park or elsewhere on wolves."

Nevertheless, in the late 1800s, market hunters and sportsmen became incensed because great numbers of wolves were slaughtering great numbers of deer in the U.P. (freely translated to mean that they didn't like this unfair competition for venison). And there is little doubt that this was essentially true. Field studies in Minnesota and Ontario showed that wolves tend to consume an average biomass of food equivalent to about 20 adult-size deer per wolf per year; or a greater number of such prey if fawns are included in the kill, as generally is the case, especially in the winter. Under unfavorable yarding conditions for deer, wolves become very efficient predators and may practice "surplus killing," i.e., they down all animals they can catch, above and beyond food needs. Shiras stated that a single wolf could destroy dozens of yarded deer within a few hours. He estimated from the carcasses found that more than 2,000 deer were killed by wolves in the vicinity of Whitefish Lake in the four years preceding 1908. No wolf always kills every deer it attacks, however, and in the absence of predators, Shiras' herd may have been doomed to serious starvation losses a few years hence, anyway. Aldo Leopold eloquently addressed this issue in his brilliant essay *Thinking Like a Mountain*. As a young forester in the Southwest he had had the opportunity to shoot wolves:

> *"We reached the old wolf in time to watch a fierce green fire dying in her eyes. I realized then... that there was something new to me in those eyes — something known only to her and to the mountain. I was young then, and full of trigger-itch; I thought that because fewer wolves meant more deer, that no wolves would mean hunters' paradise. But after seeing the green fire die, I sensed that neither the wolf nor the mountain agreed with such a view.... I now suspect that just as a deer herd lives in mortal fear of its wolves, so does a mountain live in mortal fear of its deer. And perhaps with better cause, for while a buck pulled down by wolves can be replaced in two or three years, a range pulled down by too many deer may fail of replacement in as many decades."*

Leopold was not making a moral judgment against killing wolves; rather, it suddenly dawned on him that predation is vital to the stability of a delicate (e.g., arid) ecosystem. The pendulum has now swung from one extreme — all predators are bad — to the opposite side — predators have little or no impact on game (or wildlife), whereas the truth lies somewhere in between both untenable viewpoints.

Wolves probably lingered in remote reaches of Lower Michigan until at least 1907. Research by biologist Adolph Stebler in an Alger/Schoolcraft County study in 1938 indicated that a pair of wolves with two pups had a winter range of 260 square miles, while a pack of 6 animals (4 pups) exhibited a winter range of 98 square miles in 1950 near Hulbert, in Luce County. For the most part, their winter home ranges closely coincided with deeryard boundaries, which provided a reliable food base. From early March to mid-April 1950 (6 weeks), the Hulbert pack killed 48 deer, 75 percent of whom were downed within 100 yards of the yard. Over one-half of the known kills were adult deer, which attests to the pack's efficiency as predators. Only three deer apparently escaped the wolves' charge, two of them during the melting snow of the spring break-up in April. (It is germane that wolf expert David Mech noted that under poor yarding conditions and severe winter weather, high densities of wolves actually exterminated local whitetail populations in Minnesota and Quebec.)

Stebler concluded that between 1935 and 1949 (15 years), the U.P. supported five mated pairs of wolves. In 1955 their total number was estimated to be approximately 100 wolves, which suffered an annual mortality rate of nearly 63 percent, mainly from bounty trapping. This loss equaled the population surplus via birth increment each spring. Animals presented for bounty sharply declined from around 30 annually until 1956 to only 7 in 1957 and 1958, then dropping to only a lone individual in 1959. As a consequence the existing bounty ($15 for males, $20 for females) was removed. The species received full legal protection in 1965, when only 12 - 25 wolves were believed to be present in the U.P. Some of these quite likely represented animals from Ontario crossing Whitefish Bay or the St. Marys River on the ice. Most sightings and tracks consisted of lone individuals, and recruitment evidently was nil from 1957 onward.

Why wolves suddenly disappeared from the U.P. — after having survived centuries of constant persecution — has never been adequately explained, in my opinion. Like any other animal, wolf populations invariably decline in times of food shortages. Some pups die of starvation when the parents/pack cannot provide enough food, particularly in winter. With further food restrictions, breeding ceases — even the alpha female skips her estrual cycle. Ultimately, severe intraspecific strife ensues, and subordinate animals are killed. However, the unexpected crash in wolf population after 1956 occurred while deer were still very plentiful in most sectors of the U.P. Evidently, some factor(s) other than nutrition was or were responsible. But what precisely? The "pat" answer, of course, is that they were all killed by bounty hunters. To argue persuasively that this truly occurred, however, one must show that the bounty system finally made a significant inroad into their breeding stock. But examination of available records fails to indicate that such was the case. That is, the number of wolves presented for bounty went down slightly during the last 10 years of bounties, rather than rising sharply, as should have occurred if heavy trapping pressure was responsible for their extermination in the face of normal reproductive proficiency.

Many moons ago I happened to read an erudite paper in a now unremembered journal which postulated that if wolves are subjected to serious psychological stress from close interactions with humans, they will stop breeding. Admittedly I haven't seen this intriguing concept expounded upon in recent literature on wolf behavior. To me it is quite plausible that this was a causal or predisposing element in the wolf's disappearance from the U.P. Even today, many persons persist in the delusion that the Upper Peninsula remains a bona fide "wilderness." In reality, the region's human population of 300,000 averages 20 persons per square mile, and the density skyrockets during summer tourism. Wilderness proponents have only to fly over the region at dusk to ponder, incredulously, where the myriad lights down below are coming from! What constitutes wilderness obviously rests in the eyes of the beholder. As long ago as 1952, a report prepared for the Michigan Conservation Commission stressed that "the disappearance of large tracts of wilderness areas has been responsible more than anything else [e.g., bounties] for the disappearance of the wolf" in Upper Michigan.

A study in Wisconsin indicated that wolves failed to live in areas where maintained (i.e. 2-wheel drive) roads exceeded 0.93 miles/mile$^2$ because of low human-induced survival. (A recent study suggested, however, that wolves try to avoid areas of human activity or commotion; i.e., their absence can be attributed to behavioral traits as opposed to direct attrition.) Similar findings were reported for Minnesota. Road densities in Minnesota (if not elsewhere) are therefore being restricted to less than the threshold level on public lands subject to state and federal control, comprising over 50 percent of that state's extensive wolf range (which has a more genuine wilderness character compared to Upper Michigan). Any additional improved-roads constructed for forestry or other purposes would therefore prove detrimental to local wolf populations unless these were gated to prevent incidental access, especially by off-road vehicles. Because of bountiful snow, since the early 1960s the U.P. has become a Mecca for hordes of snowmobilers from throughout the Midwest. Thus, unless the woodland travel of these enthusiasts (plus owners of ORVs and 4-WDs) was strictly limited to stipulated trails only, it might be difficult for bonded wolves to find requisite solitude during the breeding season. So much so as to discombobulate these intelligent animals and shut off their reproduction. (Skeptics ought to ponder the nature of the trance-like, or comatose, demeanor manifested by captured wolves during handling. Although this odd behavior is poorly understood for lack of study, I intuitively ascribe it to their absolute submission to man — the *summa alpha* — in terms of their social hierarchy.)

In March 1974, in an effort to augment the meager U.P. population (if any), four Minnesota wolves were released in Marquette County. All were dead by November; one was shot by a person plinking with a .22 rifle, one was caught inadvertently by a coyote trapper, one was killed by a deer hunter (mistaking it for a coyote?), and one was hit by a car; hence none of these were premeditated deaths, as some critics insinuate. On the other hand, one could argue that their habituation to attendants (i.e., loss of fear) while penned actually hastened their demise upon release into the "wild."

A few wolves occasionally enter the U.P. from Wisconsin, and probably from Ontario. Although another effort to reintroduce wolves here is not currently being advocated, the goal now is to allow the limited population to recover naturally to as many as 60 animals peninsula-wide. It is my considered opinion, however, that this obsessive endeavor will prove to be another exercise in futility, however noble the intent.[8] Sentimentality aside, wolves and humans don't mix well, except perhaps in zoos. In all likelihood, maintaining a large wolf population (recently upped to 80) across the U.P. will assuredly require stringent restrictions (even exclusion) of human activity on many hundreds (maybe thousands) of square miles of public lands — a prohibitive price in my view. Outdoor recreation is a coveted way of life for virtually all Upper Michigan residents (20 percent of whom are seniors with unlimited leisure time), and they would be loath to give up such pursuits without inciting a furor of opposition.

Nor would such a project constitute a biological imperative to save the species from extinction; witness, for example, that upwards of 50,000 - 60,000 wolves still roam the Canadian/Alaskan wilds, and their numbers evidently are increasing. Repopulation efforts could ultimately result in hybridization; a lone female wolf in heat might be compelled to mate with a large dog, thereby producing fertile offspring. Such hybrids have been noted in North America and elsewhere, e.g., Italy, USSR, Israel. Interbreeding among red wolves and dogs (or with coyotes) in the Texas/Louisiana region has also been reported. Hybrids are not protected by law in Michigan. Wolf-dog crosses must be discouraged because they pose grave danger as untrustworthy "pets." Moreover, infusing half-breed genes into pure stock warps the genotype's programmed reactions to natural situations in ways which make the animals quite unpredictable. (A recent issue of *Smithsonian* magazine reported the alarming statistics that there currently are 100,000 captive wolves and 400,000 wolf hybrids in our country, with an estimated 250,000 new [hybrid wolf-dog] pups coming to market each year. One authority concluded that "if you put these hybrid offspring together with other dogs or with people, you've got a genetic formula for disaster.") In a technical review of the present situation, The Wildlife Society recommended that reintroduction of gray (and red) wolves "should be

*After a brief, abortive effort to stock Isle Royale with tame wolves (They frightened campers!), "Queenie" was retrieved and penned with a male coyote, "Red", at the Cusino Wildlife Research Station in Shingleton. The pair mated annually for many years, but the couplings never produced pups. Although only half her size, Red completely dominated Queenie, except when a dog strayed near the pen, at which time she went berserk and he ran and hid until her rage subsided. The pair had incredibly keen hearing, being able to detect an oncoming train long before it hove into sight. They responded with an eerie acappella duet combining her mournful o o o o howl with his sharp yip, yip, yip; which at night would raise the hackles on one's neck.*

made only in areas with substantial wilderness character and adequate prey populations, where conflicts with livestock are least likely, and where local support is prevalent." For the record, the U.P. presently husbands 77,000 head of livestock, including 60,000 cattle (and calves), plus nearly equal numbers (+6,000) of sheep, swine, and horses. As Minnesota's David Mech warns, "Wolves that start colonizing agricultural areas will have to be managed, which translates to killing them where they do not belong." This surely would promote an emotional outcry from indignant, ultra-protective persons.

In recent years the Isle Royale wolf population has dropped alarmingly from a record high of 50 animals in 1980 to only 11 in the 1988-89 winter census (climbing to 15 by 1993-94). This has caused considerable consternation among National Park Service officials regarding the future wolf/moose "balance of nature" status. Four hypotheses have been advanced by Michigan Technological University biologist Rolf Peterson to explain the situation: a food shortage for wolves caused by a moose herd comprised (temporarily) of prime-age animals, the most difficult to subdue; exposure of wolves to canine parvovirus and Lyme disease; loss of genetic variability from inbreeding; and the prospects that wolves are now so few that random population or individual events may lead to extinction through inadequate reproduction. However, the four wolves captured for physical examination in 1989 had high body weights and exhibited blood parameters indicative of excellent health, suggesting that food intake was adequate during their critical developmental stage. The two adult females handled had never whelped, which is not unexpected in an alpha female-only breeding system. Food supply in 1989 was considered adequate for reproduction for one of the wolf packs, at least.

If either Lyme disease or parvovirus are indeed adversely affecting wolves on Isle Royale, then they stand little chance of existing in the U.P., where both agents are endemic, plus the fact that other virulent diseases (plus mange) are rampant in the many unvaccinated dogs running loose.

The deleterious effect of inbreeding on genetic vigor seemingly has been overstated as it concerns free-roaming animals, where natural selection ruthlessly weeds out the unfit (unlike the situation in man and domestic animals, where human sympathy keeps abnormal specimens alive to reproduce). Many viable wildlife populations once were reduced to 20 - 30 individuals (e.g. whooping cranes, California elephant seals, black-footed ferrets, red wolves, Hawaiian nene) without apparent ill-effects, since their numbers are increasing. Researcher Ulysses Seal stated in *National Wildlife* that based on present knowledge "no species is doomed unless it gets down to two or three individuals." It is noteworthy that the famed George Reserve deer herd in southern Michigan originated from the stocking of four does (presumed to be pregnant) and 2 bucks, all from Grand Island near Munising, in 1928. Within six years the herd had grown to at least 160 animals in this 1,146-acre enclosure. Over the many decades since, this herd has been studied intensively to model the population dynamics of the species. Additionally, in 1962 the MDNR stocked South Fox Island, in Lake Michigan, with 15 deer (6 males, 9 females). In 1969, hunters harvested over 37 deer/mile$^2$ during the first open (any-deer) season on this 5 square mile island. Annual hunts are being continued in an effort to keep this herd in balance with its range. There has been no hint that hereditary aberrations or congenital defects have materialized from this limited stocking. Lack of genetic diversity becomes crucial if and when profound habitat changes occur to which animals from a small gene pool cannot adjust within a short interval. Few species are so specialized as to utilize only very specific ecological niches.

It is entirely possible that out-cross breedings may have gone undetected on Isle Royale. Peterson's mentor, Durward Allen, observed 3 or 4 clearly identifiable melanistic (black) wolves visiting there in March 1967, quite likely from the Sibley Peninsula in Ontario, about 15 miles away, where this color phase is common. Allen noted that "the [resident] wolves were in a state of social chaos or at least complete disorganization." It was not known whether visiting males did any breeding; if so this could have introduced "new blood" into the presumably pure genotype (theoretically originating from one pregnant bitch) on hand initially. Allen worried whether other wolves had also visited the island unrecognized through at least 1972, as this would vitiate the assumption of a "closed" biological system.

Several years ago a pack of wolves dubbed the "gang of four" roamed Isle Royale bent on killing other wolves. Such internecine behavior provides a clue that something is seriously amiss, or socially stressful, with these animals. Summer visitors (May-September) to Isle Royale are increasing to an all-time high (more than 17,000 persons annually). Is this growing incidence of wolf/human interaction unnerving these sensitive beasts or otherwise upsetting their normal equanimity? Rolf Peterson's data revealed that wolf dens ordinarily are located more than one-half mile from established hiking trails (which presently total 174 miles in criss-crossing the island). Allen concluded that if his student's finding of spatial interactions "was a measure of [denning] requirements, then 75 percent of Isle Royale was already off limits for wolves in locating their homesites."

It might be necessary, therefore, to limit hikers in order to reduce this potential source of tension for wolves; not to mention to also perpetuate the true wilderness aura of this attractive spot.

When the deer herd increased tremendously in Ontario's Algonquin Provincial Park, wolves began to prey on them in preference to moose, which are much more difficult to kill. However, the swifter, more agile deer required a swifter, more agile type of wolf. Some Ontario biologists believe that a leaner, smaller wolf was favored through natural selection in a span of a century. Now that deer have virtually disappeared, the genetic process must work in reverse, since currently adult moose have a distinct advantage in repelling wolves. Any suggestion of infusing the existing packs with genes from larger, stronger brutes present northward would predictably bring howls of protest from the public, who probably are cheering for the moose in this case. Meanwhile the moose have saturated their range within the Park, and it will take time for Mother Nature to rectify the present predator/prey disparity.

# COYOTE

The coyote evidently was present in Lower Michigan in presettlement times, and moved northward as habitat became more favorable for them. They arrived in the U.P. after 1900. The species quickly spread, and now is found in every county. Coyotes invaded Isle Royale around 1906, but disappeared in 1957 or 1958, perhaps because of reduced food supply via competition from wolves. The wolf's penchant for killing coyotes on sight no doubt hastened their departure, however. (A Minnesota study showed that wolves also kill and eat dogs, which they may perceive as prey and deliberately hunt down.) Coyotes are common in the U.P., where few wolves exist. The "clever" coyote easily lives up to its reputation, being resourceful and opportunistic in finding enough food to thrive almost anywhere. Coyotes are antagonistic toward foxes, who must find vacant territories to avoid such interspecific strife, or face death.

# Red and Gray Fox

Red fox were present in every Michigan county, even on the larger islands within the Great Lakes, during presettlement times. The species may not have been too abundant until the forests were razed, which produced much habitat edge and led to a veritable feast from small rodents, insects, and fruiting plants forming the mainstay of their diet. Red fox do well in and around farmsteads and open vistas, areas which coyotes tend to avoid.

The gray fox occurs throughout the U.P., probably in scattered pockets; however, it is quite reclusive and rarely seen unless trapped. This animal presumably is living near the northern periphery of its natural range, and therefore exhibits major population ups and downs in the U.P. Because their ranges commonly overlap, gray foxes may be at a big disadvantage in vying for food with the more northern-adapted red fox. The gray fox is primarily a woodland creature, and its long, curved claws are suited for climbing trees (though hardly in a squirrel-like sense).

# 8

# CATS

## MOUNTAIN LION

Mountain lions (a.k.a. cougar, puma, panther) once roamed state-wide, but probably became extinct in much of Lower Michigan by the 1830s, becoming rare northward soon thereafter. Early reports did not always distinguish between mountain lions, lynx, and bobcats, and these species sometimes were lumped together and ambiguously referred to as wildcats or "catamounts." In Upper Michigan, presumably valid mountain lion records persisted into the early decades of the Twentieth Century, possibly as late as 1937 in the Huron Mountains. Mountain lions apparently were common in Wisconsin; the last specimen reportedly was killed in 1905 in Douglas County, which borders the western tip of Lake Superior.

In the early 1950s, numerous newspaper reports told of sightings of a "phantom cat," mainly from the vicinity of Pickford, south of the Sault. The animal in question invariably was large, tawny in color, with a long tail—which certainly fits the description of a mountain lion. These sightings usually came in bunches, but from disparate locations; such distribution strongly implicates the power of suggestion in prompting hallucinations among susceptible observers. Occasional sightings "indisputably" of mountain lions still persist today, but now come mainly from the central U.P. However, no less an authority than Rollin Baker remarked:

*"Mammalogists have yet [1983] to examine a specimen, an authentic footprint, or even view a photograph of the animal. It should be remembered that although the mountain lion, in spite of its large size, is most secretive in its actions, it will (1) leave numerous tracks and other characteristic signs, and (2) periodically need to make a kill, either a white-tailed deer or a head of domestic stock, using identifiable feline techniques including the caching of uneaten portions. Consequently, its presence cannot escape detection for long… One of these animals would certainly have been shot, treed by hounds, or trapped, if actually present."*

These animals have distinctive paw prints and drag their tails in deep snow, yet its spoor has never been reported in winter, and we know it doesn't hibernate! A study in Idaho showed that a mountain lion may kill up to a couple dozen deer (their mainstay food) per year. This number of partially-eaten, leaf-covered carcasses surely would not long escape detection by the swarms of woodsworkers, sportsmen, or hikers in our region.

Reports of mountain lions in the East increased from the late 1940s onward, coincident with increased coverage in the popular press. According to a recent study, "such reports and assertions contributed to listing of the eastern mountain lion as endangered...although there was no physical evidence of self-sustaining populations." The study concluded that reported sighting (or tracks) by themselves "should never serve as a basis for describing the distribution or abundance of mountain lions." (The same caveat likewise applies to purported sightings/tracks of wolves.)

This is not to say that a stray animal will not reach the U.P. by sheer chance. Mountain lions, especially juvenile males, often travel great distances in search of living space outside the territories of established alpha males. To reach Michigan from the nearest population in the Rocky Mountains, however, a mountain lion would have to cross extensive expanses of open, thickly settled countryside, where it could readily be seen. It seems safe to conclude that a viable (i.e., reproducing) population of mountain lions does not presently exist in Upper Michigan — despite (the absurdity of) legal protection. Nevertheless, a tame animal may eventually be released here, as has been the case with wolf/dog hybrids in recent years. Hartley Jackson noted that any record of a puma in Wisconsin since 1920 probably involves animals which either escaped or were released as unwanted pets by automobile travelers. Amen!

*Like the wolverine, the lynx has a circumpolar distribution, ranging throughout the boreal forest and northward into the tundra. Its comparatively long legs and oversize paws enable this animal to traverse powdery snow with ease. Periodic population highs in Canada cause young lynx to seek uninhabited areas, even reaching Upper Michigan. (Lynn Rogers.)*

# LYNX AND BOBCAT

The lynx formerly was found throughout Michigan, but disappeared even in the U.P. by the early 1930s. Its fur is highly prized, and it is relatively easily trapped. Northward the lynx is closely tied to cyclic snowshoe hare populations in the classical predator/prey interrelationship. The lynx undoubtedly evolved in a boreal ecosystem in which it needed oversize paws to match the "satchel" feet of hares in traversing the powdery snowpack typical

*The secretive, usually nocturnal bobcat is rarely sighted, and therefore is erroneously considered rare. Their preferred habitat is a dense conifer swamp, where small mammals as well as deer are generally plentiful. The harvest of bobcats is closely controlled, thus assuring a stable U.P. population, except where their habitat is being destroyed. (Lynn Rogers.)*

of arctic environments. Stray lynx visit the U.P. from time to time. A rash of scattered records surfaced in the early 1960s; 12 animals (lawfully protected) were taken incidentally in 1962. These probably represented temporal immigrants from Canada, which experienced peak lynx densities during that period. Despite legal sanctuary, it seems unlikely that lynx will ever again be common in this region.

Long ago the lynx was replaced/displaced by the bobcat, who benefitted from the felling of U.P. forests. The young stands of mixed timber that regenerated favored a greater variety and abundance of small mammals (as well as deer) which bobcats favor as food. The denser, readily compacted snowpack found in the U.P. (due to the ameliorating "lake-effect" weather) serves to minimize the advantage enjoyed by the lynx in running down prey where fluffy snow is the rule overwinter. George Shiras thought that bobcats increased from nil to numerous within his lifetime, whereas lynx numbers diminished sharply in the Marquette area. He noted that state-employed trappers captured 126 bobcats and 15 lynx in northern Michigan in 1928, and felt that these figures gave a good indication of the relative abundance of the two animals. Reportedly, where lynx and bobcat coexist, the latter seems more aggressive in expressing agonistic behavior. If so, perhaps the two species were not meant to live together amicably. Bobcat populations appear to be stable in the U.P.; their harvest is being closely watched to prevent any decline in numbers.

*The lone extant specimen of a Michigan wolverine consists of this animal known to have been taken in the Vanderbilt/Gaylord area in the late 1860s, and mounted by naturalist Charles Davis of Lansing. It is now owned by Gary Kaberle of Traverse City, being part of an extensive collection of Davis' mounts inherited from his grandfather. Hopefully this photo will put an end to the inane polemics concerning the true legitimacy of the "Wolverine State."*

# 9

# WOLVERINES *ET AL.*

## WOLVERINE

Periodically, presumably on a "slow" news day, the media resurrects the perennial argument about whether Michigan really should be called the Wolverine State. It is true that there are no Michigan study skins or skulls preserved in university museums, nor have any bones been dug up as irrefutable evidence that wolverines once roamed here. Nevertheless, a mounted specimen exists from an animal known to have been taken in downstate Otsego County in the late 1860s. The state's zoologist reported in 1860 that the wolverine is "seldom found in the Lower Peninsula, having been nearly exterminated" by then in this region. Legendary biologist Vernon Bailey described the fabled brute as "an animal of the solitudes, shunning human occupation, vanishing with the spread of civilization."

A story in the Milwaukee *Daily Wisconsin* dated March 20, 1860, told about a strange animal being caught in a trap by a person living near Marquette:

*It was about three and a half or four feet long, with black legs and head, with rather coarse hair, resembling that of a bear; reddish color on the sides, and dark brown on the belly, with whitish spots on the head; head small, something like an anteater's, nose pointed, tail short and bushy, legs short but very large, with claws like a bear. Nobody seemed to know anything about it, although one person spoke of seeing the same description of animal on the coast of Labrador, and that there the French call it 'carcajou'. He also described them as possessing great strength and as being for their cunning much dreaded by trappers."*

Mammalogist William Burt noted that this account described the wolverine better than any other animal that lived in our region. The species probably occurred throughout Michigan, and there are authentic records of its presence in 7 U.P. counties and 10 counties in the northern L.P.

A wolverine reportedly was captured near Champion in the 1880s; one was killed by trappers in Schoolcraft County in October 1879 because it was raiding their trapline. Another individual was sighted crossing the Menominee River in 1871. An old settler recalled seeing wolverine in the Huron Mountains until 1903. Wolverines were uncommon but existed throughout Wisconsin in presettlement days; authority Hartley Jackson lists ten valid records for that state. The last animal reportedly was killed in 1932 in Iron County, which borders the U.P.; thus the species surely existed in the Wolverine State at some earlier date. There is evidence that it once lived in Indiana. But surprisingly, there are no positive records of wolverines within a hundred miles of Sault Ste. Marie, Ontario. However, there is a mounted specimen in the Royal Ontario Museum reportedly taken in the Bruce Peninsula, although one authority questions the venue, for unspecified reasons.

Wolverines, especially juvenile males, are great travelers; a wanderlust specimen even turned up in Iowa in 1961. Like all mustelids, wolverines defend a fixed territory against encroachment by others of the same sex; males typically have larger territories than females. Assuming that U.P. wolverines historically occurred at a density of one animal per 77 or 163 square miles, as in Montana and British Columbia, respectively, the few individuals present locally at a given time could readily have been trapped out without any documentation forthcoming. The fact that wolverine pelts were brought to Michigan trading posts from far-off lands is of academic interest only, and not really relevant to the central issue. Hopefully a wolverine skull or some identifiable bones will be uncovered in a marl deposit or peat bog to convince even die-hard skeptics that the species indisputably was part of our native fauna.

# MARTEN AND FISHER

The marten formerly was found in all counties of the U.P., but became extinct because massive habitat changes occurred, plus overharvest. The last known record was from the Huron Mountains in 1940. The Michigan DNR's first effort to re-establish the marten in Michigan was made during the winters of 1954-55 and 1955-56, when 29 animals obtained in Ontario from wild and penned stock were released in the Porcupine Mountains State Park. A few of these animals lived until 1962, after which there were no reliable reports of tagged specimens or tracks near the release site. In the winters of 1968-69 and 1969-70, 99 marten (62 males, 37 females) live-trapped in Ontario were

*The marten has been restored to its former U.P. haunts by liberating animals captured in Ontario. It is a very agile, efficient predator, and a valuable furbearer. Like other mustelids, this normally shy animal becomes a snarling fury when provoked.*

released in the Whitefish River area north of Rapid River. These animals were purchased through the auspices of the U.S. Forest Service. Their cooperation in this venture was not altogether altruistic; marten are the main predator of red squirrels, which in turn have a great affinity for conifer seed. Too many red squirrels mean not enough seed for natural conifer regeneration; ergo, red squirrels must be controlled to benefit forest management!

The second marten restocking effort was successful, as affirmed by recovery of untagged injured or car-killed specimens shortly thereafter, plus reliable sightings and tracks of marten far from the release site. All adult females presumably were pregnant when released in March, and would have given birth in April (following a long interval of delayed implantation of the blastocysts), thus yielding untagged specimens. Nonetheless, owing to poor communications, another "reintroduction" attempt was carried out from 1978 to 1981, involving various cooperating agencies. The 148 marten, again from Ontario, were released in selected areas (mainly stocked with mature timber) in the western half of the U.P. At about the same time, Wisconsin released some of them just across the Michigan border. The marten has spread into all suitable habitats, of which there seemingly are many throughout the U.P. Some animals have been live-trapped for restocking the northern Lower Peninsula.

The fisher was native to Upper Michigan and most of the Lower Peninsula. However, the Biennial Report of 1933-34 noted that it was practically extinct in the U.P. (much earlier below the Mackinac Straits). Beginning in 1956, fishers were obtained from populations in New York and Ontario for release in the Nicolet and Chequamegon National Forest as part of a joint venture between the Wisconsin DNR and the U.S. Forest Service. In another such endeavor with the Michigan DNR, fishers were released in the Ottawa National Forest. Through April 1963, 122 specimens (84 males, 38 females) were liberated. By the early 1970s, the fisher population was thriving and spreading in all directions.

Aside from the biological desirability of returning a species to its former haunts, the fisher was imported

*Despite its formidable array of sharp quills, the porcupine is defenseless against those who take umbrage at the animal's fondness for tree cambium and its taste for salt. Porkies have few natural enemies except the fisher, which at least comes down to a fair fight.*

expressly (if tacitly) to control porcupines, which have long been the bane of foresters because of their predilection for feeding on dominant and codominant trees, often girdling the tops (a sin for which they were shot on sight!). The fisher is the only mammal that can consistently kill porcupines without getting a mouthful of painful — often lethal — quills. (It repeatedly bites the porkie's face until the victim dies from this trauma or suffocates, then "peels" open the belly skin like an orange to reach the flesh.) The project was very successful, as there clearly appear to be far fewer porcupines around now compared to three or four decades ago. (This is not entirely a big plus, since this lumbering creature is a captivating, if sometimes vexing, part of our fauna, and not a prolific one.) Snowshoe hares constitute a favorite food of fisher, which attests to its quickness in outrunning such fleet prey. Given the apparent sharp decline in U.P. wood-chucks in recent years, perhaps fishers also dine regularly on that animal.

Reportedly the marten prefers old-growth coniferous habitat, but will utilize other timber types if food is plentiful; hence they often can be found in lightly cut-over northern hardwoods or mixed stands. In contrast, the fisher is not so limited by forest characteristics, and prospers in a wider assortment of environments. These differences, plus dissimilarities in size of prey hunted, probably comprise evolutionary adaptations which permit both species to coexist without undue interspecific competition. Both mustelids are deemed easy to trap, however; hence their populations must be monitored closely to avoid overexploitation. The Michigan DNR has authorized a limited trapping season on fisher in the U.P. to utilize surplus animals, as well as to "salvage" pelts taken in traps set for other species. (Trappers are now required to buy a "fur harvester" license — a euphemism for the more coldblooded connotation.)

# OTTER AND BADGER

The otter was present throughout the state when the white man came, but it was extirpated from the southern tier of counties by the early 1900s. They persisted at low levels in the northern part of Michigan. In 1925 the otter was granted complete legal protection. In 1940 the Department of Conservation was accorded full discretionary authority to manage otter (and beaver). By virtue of conservative rules in setting seasons and bag limits, otter populations rebounded to the point of abundance in at least the forested two-thirds of Michigan.

Otters are highly territorial, thus there will never be a great number of these animals in a given locale even without legal trapping. Contrary to the protestations of trout fishermen, otter do not have much impact on game fish populations except, perhaps, in special circumstances (e.g., at hatcheries). They devour a variety of prey, including so-called trash fish, many of which compete directly with trout for aquatic forage. When otters become too numerous, their populations can readily be controlled by trapping.

Although ungainly out of water, otter commonly make long overland trips, seemingly oblivious to possible predation; but they no doubt are formidable opponents when cornered. While otter young may become independent by autumn, family groups (mother and kits) sometimes

*In early times the otter was found throughout Michigan, but its present range is limited to the northern two-thirds of the state, where it exists in good numbers. It is a graceful, powerful swimmer; hence it can easily catch fish, too easily in the eyes of sorehead anglers! Otters seemingly are born to play, and thereby "enjoy" life more than any other mammal except, perhaps, man. (Lynn Rogers.)*

remain together through winter. They make a memorable sight when seen fishing through holes in the ice at such time. (For those who look forward to reincarnation, the fun-loving otter would be a good choice by which to return to planet Earth. I for one would enjoy sliding belly-first down a slippery slope into a pool!)

Although the badger has been recorded from every county in Upper Michigan, it is rarely sighted. I have seen specimens only once, a mother and two kits killed by a car at dusk near Limestone nearly 30 years ago. Additional badgers have been reported within the past few years in the southcentral U.P., and even near Marquette; the possible reason for this apparent increase is uncertain, but may be in response to a succession of mild winters. The species presumably entered the U.P. from Wisconsin (which, according to Hartley Jackson, was dubiously dubbed the Badger State) in the early part of this century, after much of the forestland had been cleared. They prefer open areas covered by grass or low shrubs, and seemingly avoid heavily wooded sites, where requisite clear visibility is notably lacking. Badgers are prodigious diggers, but I have yet to find any evidence of such fossorial activity even when purposely looking for it.

The badger evolved in association with the thirteen-lined ground squirrel, its favorite prey. In the U.P. this spermophile has been found only as far east as Marquette County, and nowhere is it present in large numbers. Badgers are also fond of woodchucks, which are common around farmland and clearings throughout the region. It also scavenges on carrion. They require ample food intake in autumn in order to store enough body fat for winters

inanition, and invoke a physiologic mechanism which enables them to survive in a semi-torpid state. One worker found that the animal spent up to 70 days in its burrow during cold weather. Females give birth as early as late March, by which time there still may be considerable snow on the ground; one mother did not leave her litter for seven days after parturition to search for food.

Given their extremely low density in any one area, and the widely scattered distribution of individual home ranges, the wonder is that they somehow manage to reproduce. Certainly inbreeding must be common within a particular cell of such isolated groups. Whether lack of genetic diversity is keeping badger populations at minimal levels is, of course, speculative, but worthy of special study.

# 10

# BEAVERS AND BEARS

It hardly seems possible that a homely workaholic whose pelage is not nearly as luxuriant as that of other furbearers was largely responsible for the frenzied activity characterizing the early fur trade in North America. The Indians trapped the beaver for its hide and meat, and used its sinews, teeth, bones, and other organs for a variety of survival and cultural needs. There is no reason to think that they overexploited the animal until the white man induced them to do so. The French explorers began trading decorative objects and utensils, cloth, and guns for beaver pelts obtained by the Indians. The fur was used to make felt hats then much in style among European gentry. In fact, the British Parliament proclaimed in 1638 that only beaver fur was to be used to manufacture some hats. And trap beaver they did; in 1767 alone, for example, 50,938 hides were shipped from Fort Michilimackinac to England. However, most of these beaver doubtless were not trapped locally, since this trading post served as a collecting point for skins from far away places. After 1830, beaver hats went out of fashion, which saved the species from almost certain extinction.

Michigan's beaver population remained low (or absent locally) for decades following its nadir density. The state imposed closed seasons between 1920 and 1930 in an effort to keep them from being wiped out. Biologists were given discretionary authority to manage beaver by Legislative act in 1940. Beaver populations increased greatly as a result, and the animals now are found in all counties except extreme southeastern and southwestern Michigan. The annual beaver take varies according to prevailing fur prices, which were exceptionally high soon after WWII (a "dollar-an-inch," referring to diameter for pelts stretched round), but have since fallen sharply. Most beaver currently are taken by "recreational" trappers who make very little money from such pastime activities. Locally beavers may be overabundant, causing serious flooding of roads, railways, or timber. Fishermen often vociferously complain that after the first few years beaver dams are a detriment on trout streams, claiming that the impounded water is warmed beyond the fish's tolerance. (These quiet ponds are attractive to a host of unique animal and plant species, however, as well as to man.) High beaver populations sometimes are subject to disease outbreaks. They were decimated by tularemia in Michigan and neighboring states in 1952-55; cottontails and snowshoe hares are similarly afflicted. Tularemia also proved deadly for humans —including a Michigan game pathologist — when contracted prior to the advent of antibiotics.

In the pristine setting, beaver populations generally were low because aspen, their staple food, was in limited

*Where aspen is plentiful, beaver may build gigantic lodges, adding pieces to it after eating the bark. Beaver populations in Upper Michigan have rebounded from nadir levels probably to an all-time high owing to abundant food supply through forest management favoring aspen production. However, because of low fur prices, hence minimal trapping effort, in many areas beaver have become serious pests by flooding roads and timber.*

*Beavers can grow to mammoth size, upwards of 100 pounds, which provide sought-after "blanket" pelts of highest value. Most beavers (and other aquatic furbearers) are currently taken in Conibear-type traps which kill instantly, or in drowning sets.*

abundance along streams. Once an aspen supply had been harvested, the site converted to the climax type, and the local beavers had to move on to find new sources. (Some biologists believe that sharply reduced beaver populations with advent of the fur trade influenced forest ecology through non-maintenance/construction of dams, whose backwater promote distinctive plant communities through biochemical processes.) Intensive logging today generally assures the perpetuation in place of secondary plant succession featuring aspen. In many localities, therefore, beaver populations will continue at current high, often

nuisance, levels. Although beaver have historically been heralded as masterful engineers, they often blunder in selecting dam sites, some of which repeatedly wash out in times of high water. Many beaver use bank burrows in lieu of lodges if streams or rivers are too large to dam or are otherwise unsuitable (as is the case with lakes). Animals occupying marginal habitats are forced to use tree and shrub species which provide poor nutrition, leading to a tenuous existence for an individual or colony.

Once present throughout Michigan, the black bear is now largely restricted in its distribution to the northern

*As in all mammals, adequate nutritional resources promote early fertility and high fecundity for female black bears. Biologists now track them to their winter dens via radiotelemetry to check on the occupants. Even when she feels threatened, a mother almost always bluffs an attack on humans. Almost always! (Lynn Rogers.)*

two-thirds of the state. Perhaps as could be predicted, the species is thriving in the "wilds" of Upper Michigan. Although bears always were common here, the nutritional welfare of this omnivore quite likely benefitted greatly from logging of the virgin forests. Creation of innumerable clearings, rotting logs, etc., produced a virtual supermarket of fruiting plants and insects that are the mainstay of a bear's diet. Access to winter-killed deer provides vital nourishment for lean bears after they leave their dens in spring. They are in the habit of dining on newborn whitetails, which they probably find by scent, since bruin does not possess especially good vision. A seemingly clumsy bear can run surprisingly fast for a short distance, being able to outsprint highly mobile month-old fawns.

Compared to other large mammals, bears are not very prolific breeders. Their reproductive rate depends greatly on nutrition. Females generally do not become sexually mature until at least 3.5 years old, but may reach twice that age before ovulating if food is lacking. A sow breeds in alternate years, skipping estrus while she is lactating. Bears make good mothers in defending their young, however; the only natural predators of any consequence in Michigan (excluding a rare wolf) are adult male bears, which cannibalize cubs should the chance arise.

In recent years the biology and ecology of the black bear has been studied in detail over most of its North American range. Little was known about this animal (aside from *Goldilocks*) until colleague Albert Erickson began a pioneer investigation in 1952 at the Cusino Wildlife Research Station. This required capturing free-roaming animals, for which no suitable techniques had yet been devised. Initially bears were caught in a "culvert trap" designed by the Park Service to translocate nuisance animals. Trapped bears had to be anesthetized in order to ear-tag them and obtain physical data, however. The only effective means of immobilization then was to spray medicinal ether into a more-or-less airtight (caulked) culvert trap until the animal was drugged. How this highly volatile substance never exploded and sent the workers into orbit was pure luck. Injections of pentobarbital sodium ("truth serum") was also used to anesthetize bears, especially those caught in foot-hold traps. Biologists presently have a wide array of potent yet safe drugs for immobilizing bears and other critters, which makes such work much easier and less stressful to both man and beasts.

Over a ten-year period, Erickson captured 159 different bears which were handled a total of 182 times. He estimated that the bear density in his Alger/Schoolcraft County study area around Shingleton averaged approximately 1 animal per 3.5 square miles. Extrapolation from this figure (always risky) yields a total U.P. population of roughly 4,500 animals in the mid-1950's; a plausible "ball-park figure." (Despite years of concerted research to develop reliable census techniques, we still are unable to precisely determine the number of animals within a given area for species large and small.)

Because of better nutrition, bears feeding in garbage dumps were found to have higher fecundity than free-roaming animals. Many of these almost tame garbage dump bears were shot when they became serious pests. Fortunately, the unsanitary and unsightly village dumps were legally closed a few years ago, which eliminated the public health problem as well as nuisance complaints. Cubs now are lawfully protected from hunting, which benefits the population. The current widespread practice of baiting bears prior to and during the open season quite likely enhances a sow's fecundity on next estrus.[9] Bears are now considered a "trophy" species, and as such are subject to increasing hunting pressure. However, their harvest is being closely regulated to assure stable numbers of this important big-game animal; in fact, their density may be increasing as a result.

# EPILOGUE

*How oft against the sunset sky or moon*
*We watched the moving zig-zag of spread wing*
*In unforgotten autumns gone too soon,*
*In unforgotten springs!*

**–Frederick Peterson**
*Wild Geese*

So ends my brief look backward into the life and times of Hiawatha's brothers, as I've been able to reconstruct the events based on the meager information from yesteryear. Hiawatha and I had much in common. We both learned about our four-footed brethren at an early age. He, of course, was tutored by expert kin, whereas I gleaned most of my animal lore from scholarly books. My education about wild things began while just a tyke, through reading the delightful tales in *Bedtime Stories* by Thornton W. Burgess. I was enthralled by the real-life antics of his anthropomorphic characters. Later on the writings of Ernest Thompson Seton and John Burroughs were prized. Eventually, via a very circuitous route, I perused the landmark book *Game Management,* by Aldo Leopold, and knew instantly how I wanted to spend the rest of my life.

I grew up on a farm, and as often as possible between endless chores, I'd slip into the wondrous woods behind the barn just to fool around enjoying Nature, and later to seek solace from the vicissitudes of adolescence. Like Hiawatha, I too was born to be a *cacciatore* — a hunter — it was in my blood. Despite millennia of evolution toward a quasi-civilized facade, I managed to retain a strong atavistic killer-instinct. Hiawatha's indoctrination as a hunter was out of sheer necessity — he had to slay game so his family could eat. (Yet I'll bet he also got great satisfaction in

*The author literally cut-his-teeth reading the captivating antics of wild creatures in* Bedtime Stories *by Thornton W. Burgess, a gifted writer and perceptive naturalist. In this scene, Paddy and Mrs. Beaver watch from the safety of their pond as Yowler the Bobcat wisely decides to pass up what at first glance seems like an easy meal. Upon further scrutiny the intended victim turns out to be Prickly Porky, swimming ashore (buoyed by numerous air-filled quills) after resting on the mid-pond beaver lodge. (Platt and Munk Co. Inc.)*

*The ruffed grouse can make 5-G turns while flying at ballistic speed through a thicket without so much as mussing a feather. This specimen, "Charlie," lived his life in a de facto sanctuary and became almost tame. Although reaching a ripe old age for a grouse, Charlie didn't pass on his maladaptive genes to his presumably numerous offspring. He could mesmerize people by playfully flying at them from nearby cover. (Michigan Department Natural Resources.)*

outsmarting the wary red buck, for example, much as I do.) Hiawatha used primitive implements to hunt for food; a wood bow and flint-tipped arrows, occasionally a lance, plus ingenious snares and deadfalls. In marked contrast, I use finely-crafted firearms and accessories. Sometimes he also took a dog along to help track or rout quarry. (Although Indians considered dog meat a delicacy, I've never thought of eating my Llewellyn setter, Bandit, even after those outings afield when I had to severely admonish him for gross ineptitude or rank insubordination.)

As did all my boyhood chums during the Great Depression, I hunted and trapped for the fun of it (competition), to add variety to the dinner menu, and to earn money to buy otherwise unobtainable staples or frivolous gear. Barely a teenager, I'd sleep fitfully on the eve of the small game season, fearful of missing the first light of dawn on this momentous occasion. Plinking with a .22 rifle and shooting at varmints gave me a proficiency in using guns that later came in handy as a Marine rifleman on Iwo Jima.

When I hired on as a game biologist and was sent "up north" to do deer research, I could scarcely believe my good fortune. In the inimitable words of Red Skelton, it "felt like I had died and gone to heaven!" In retrospect, my work was all-consuming and extremely gratifying, with research interest ranging from masked shrews to moose.[10] It was pretty heady stuff for a country boy, and these exciting years went by in a blur. I married a soft-hearted lady having great compassion for all life, even noxious creepy-crawlers (Aw, the poor things!). By comparison she would make arch-preservationist Albert Schweitzer seem like Attila the Hun.[11] Early on she would see me off on a hunting trip saying, "Have a good time, but I hope you don't shoot anything." Luckily, she soon developed a gourmet's taste for upland game birds. I taught her the names of wildlife we encountered and all their secrets. These creatures enriched our lives immensely, particularly on blustery winter days when our world was white with snow and the only sign of life was the shuttling of "dickey-birds" to and from their feeders.

I've reached the age when I ought to be less impassioned about life's slings and arrows, and to some extent I have mellowed, though probably not nearly enough. If Hiawatha could return to the U.P. today, he would be astonished, wondering where all these light-skinned people had come from, and what were they doing here, anyway! I can appreciate his dismay. For in my short lifetime I've seen the population of the U.S.A. more than double, to over a quarter-billion, a density which is beginning to severely restrict our "elbow-room" in the great outdoors.[12]

I always enjoy going hunting, but now the ambiance of a glorious autumn day means more to me than game in the bag (yet admittedly I hate getting "skunked"). I still tense-up seeing Bandit on point, immobile, with a side glance that seems to say, "Here he is, boss, now don't miss another easy shot, eh!" Regrettably I'm losing the good hand/eye coordination of my youth, and the lightning reflexes needed to react violently when a ruffed grouse explodes at my feet and hurtles away in twisting flight. Alas, now most of them get away unscathed. Happily the challenge to win these contests still endures.[13]

Bandit and I are growing old together, albeit at different rates. When he dies I shall have buried my last bird dog. And all too soon it will be time for my requiem; no more musings from an irascible old man. Hopefully I will then embark, like Hiawatha putting to sea in his canoe, on a long and distant journey to the Land of the Hereafter. Perchance to my Happy Hunting Grounds in the company of my venerable sportsmen ancestors.

Home is the hunter
Home from the hills.

*Few sights are more pleasing to avid bird hunters than finding their dog locked on point. And dogs make nice companions, too, adding immeasurably to the ambience of a dazzling autumn day afield. My setter Bandit is the product of centuries of selective breeding in an effort to enhance the breed's pointing instinct and physical prowess. His main shortcoming is chronic hearing impairment; the ear wax periodically has to be cleaned out by mild electro-shock therapy.*

# FOOTNOTES

1    In preparing a detailed map of presettlement forests in Upper Michigan based on his knowledge of soil characteristics, J.O. Veatch, professor emeritus of Michigan State University, ascribed to some major pine types a stocking mainly of red and jack pine, with variable amounts of white pine. While this appraisal doubtless is generally correct, it seemingly was influenced by the need to produce a broad map encompassing the entire state. In contrast, Veatch's more detailed soil maps of Alger and Schoolcraft counties, for example, indicate that the bulk of the huge Kingston Plains/Fox River Plains/Danaher Plains complex actually consisted mainly of white pine, even on the relatively poor-quality soils such as the Rubicon Sand series. This is borne out by the high stocking of readily identifiable (fluted) white pine stumps persisting on many of these sites. Red pine did in fact predominate on the drier, excessively-drained soils (e.g. the Grayling Sand series) more commonly found in northern Lower Michigan.    Pg.24

2    Not surprisingly, some scientists have challenged this hypothesis, claiming that the original study was flawed by biased sampling (i.e., improper selection) of test subjects. It would seem, however, that valid data from such research must entail physiological examinations restricted to persons of pure aboriginal lineage whose ancestors had never imbibed alcohol so as to produce "resistant" strains among surviving progeny. Subjects fulfilling these criteria would be virtually impossible to find today. Alcoholism among Indians, some authorities contend, is essentially a sociologic problem stemming from cultural/spiritual deprivation, as opposed to an organic predisposition. On the other hand, the majority of Orientals (progenitors of Indians) carry a mutant gene that makes it difficult for them to efficiently metabolize alcohol. Also, recent studies indicate that sons (if not also daughters) of alcoholics are four times more likely to follow in their parents' footsteps despite being raised in non-drinking homes. Hereditary traits or environmental stressors? The jury is still out.    Pg.38

3    It would be exceedingly naive to believe that in crossing the ice-bridge from Asia to North America the migrating Indians were miraculously shorn of attendant pathogens which thereby enabled them to live completely disease-free until they became contaminated by invading Europeans. To the contrary, scientific evidence indicates that "Without question, respiratory diseases, dysentery, and other ailments joined tuberculosis and perhaps treponemal disease to produce considerable morbidity in the pre-Columbian New World." Historians now conclude that incidents of sudden grave illness evident among Columbus' crew were attributable to outbreaks of venereal and other infectious diseases, internal parasites, etc., contracted from Indians to which the Caucasians had no immunity for lack of prior exposure. Although its epidemiology remains a subject of controversy among scholars, there is a substantial basis for believing that syphilis (caused by a spirochete bacterium *Treponema*) was brought to Europe by returning explorers, where it soon became a scourge to humanity.    Pg.39

4    In the latter instance, trees were cut into 4-foot lengths, and piled in mounds called pits (for reasons unknown) measuring up to 30 feet in diameter and 8-10 feet high, and of 25-30 cords capacity. These mounds were covered with wet leaves or sod, and kindled for several days until the gaseous distillates were driven off, leaving only a thousand or so bushels of charred wood. (This energy-wasteful and air-polluting process is still used in developing countries, where timber is in short supply, to produce charcoal fuel vital for cooking and heating.    Pg.56

FOOTNOTES

5    Although Hatcher estimated that approximately 330,000 acres of hardwoods were logged to supply charcoal for U.P. blast furnaces, LaFayette pegs the figure at 166,666 acres. I puzzled over this exactly two-fold difference, but finally decided that the disparity between workers originated from their individual interpretation of available data. That is, Hatcher based his computations on the amount of charcoal needed to **smelt** a ton of iron ore, which contained roughly 50 percent impurities, whereas LaFayette construed the matter as being the fuel required to **produce** a ton of pig iron — a notable difference in semantics. Given that all furnaces ultimately shut down from lack of charcoal, it hardly seems likely to me that just three units — namely Schoolcraft, Onota, and Fayette — alone could account for over one-half (72,000 acres) of the total cutting acreage arrived at by LaFayette. Based on the iron tonnage smelted at Fayette, fueling that operation in itself entailed razing 45,000 - 60,000 acres of hardwoods, depending upon method of computation. If indeed one acre yielded 1,000 bushels of charcoal, sufficient to produce 5 tons of pig iron, then it would have required approximately 400,000 acres of timber to make the ± 2,000,000 tons of iron cast throughout the U.P. from 1848 to 1898. For this reason, I chose Hatcher's assessment of the situation as being the more realistic appraisal of timber area logged for pig iron production.          Pg.58

6    More importantly, moreover, the same circumstances previously took place almost everywhere east of the Mississippi. One wonders what effect the tremendous release of carbon dioxide, as the vast ancient forests went up in smoke, then had on global warming via the greenhouse effect. Most of this gas presumably dissolved in water or was used directly by terrestrial vegetation (forest regeneration and agricultural crops) for increased photosynthetic activity. Interestingly, settlement brought forth innumerable livestock, and deer, who produce methane ($CH_4$), also known as marsh gas, as a product of rumen fermentation; cattle may expel (by belching) roughly 14 cubic feet of methane a day. Molecule for molecule, $CH_4$ has 20 - 30 times the greenhouse potential of carbon dioxide; unlike $CO_2$, it is not recycled in the atmosphere. Of crucial importance to the prospects for global warming is the fact that

the number of cattle world-wide is increasing faster than the human population; probably in concert with slash-and-burn agricultural practices in tropical rain forests.          Pg.74

7    Contrary to the shrill protestations of misguided environmentalists, there is nothing intrinsically bad in using the clearcutting system to regenerate certain forest types for which there is no ecological alternative. If properly done, the resultant stands will be as good as, if not better than, the one it replaced. Foresters in Europe, the cradle of scientific timber management, routinely employ clearcutting for optimum wood (and wildlife) production, even on Alp mountainsides! Conversely, although partial, or selection, cutting may seem to be a better method, if improperly applied (e.g., "take the best and leave the rest") it can drastically harm timber quality. So great are the demands for quick profit that many privately-owned forests are severely over-cut. All too frequently these lands are then placed under Commercial Forest Reserve status to avoid paying *ad valorem* taxes until the stands again reach some semblance of merchantability decades later.          Pg.75

8 Rudyard Kipling stipulated that "No talk shall be of dogs when wolf and gray wolf meet." In composing this text I agonized over the prospect of being branded a heretic (or worse) by my peers for not wholeheartedly embracing the current bandwagon espousing a wolf restoration effort in the U.P. In defense of my unpopular stance, however, I'm left with no alternative if one is to view the matter with cold professional objectivity. I admire wolves for what they truly are or ought to represent: voracious carnivores epitomizing wildness and wilderness. Admittedly I do not countenance the reverent anthropomorphic nonsense extolling their familial/sociologic virtues *ad nauseam*. I am convinced that packs of wolves roaming Upper Michigan (the southern tip of their North American range) are a thing of the past; regrettable, perhaps, but nonetheless a fact of life. In describing how politics and popular misconceptions about wolves may rule their fate in Alaska, veteran wildlife biologist Robert Stephenson summed up his considered conclusions: "Well-meaning people are spending precious time and emotion to 'save' the wolf while the species has already been 'saved.' As a result, part of

our country's environmental concern is being squandered." I concur with that conviction. Regrettably, the wolf has now become a venerated icon—a saint—in the minds of those trying to justify having one in their back yard. Pg.98

9    Deer hunting today similarly has been revolutionized by the almost universal practice of enticing them to the vicinity of shooting blinds with tempting baits. Literally tens of thousands of tons of tasty and nutritious farm produce are now set out for deer each year beginning in early autumn and replenished through the hunting season, which extends through the month of December for archery. The sum effect of this artificial feeding is to raise the fertility/fecundity of does, while maximizing fetal development by delaying or reducing the severe physiological drain usually experienced during late pregnancy in a severe winter. Hence, all bets are off insofar as predicting population trends based on criteria used before baiting became commonplace, and where many deer are being hand-fed throughout the winter! Pg.116

10    Like most of my colleagues I also dabbled in non-game wildlife affairs long before some species were declared rare and endangered. Although census/restoration activities for these animals could not legitimately be funded with hunters' monies (license fees and excise taxes), some of these endeavors were considered urgent or vital, and therefore were tacitly approved. The survival of Kirtland's warbler, for example, depended upon our provision of requisite breeding habitat (sapling jack pines) under the guise of doing habitat improvement for game animals like deer and sharptail grouse. The general public, and anti-hunters in particular, must realize that any restrictions on hunting opportunities will adversely impact certain plants and wildlife species which currently prosper only because of funded range management for specific game animals. In short, it would be folly to kill the goose that lays the golden egg!

Since 1934, hunters have been required to purchase a federal Migratory Bird Hunting Stamp to take waterfowl. To date, over 300 million dollars have been collected through this so-called "duck stamp" to

purchase (hence preserve) over 3.7 million acres of wetlands. Later, these originally-labelled *waterfowl* refuges were renamed "wildlife" refuges because they harbored numerous other animal species, some of them on the verge of extinction. The biota of these sites lures the public like a magnet, although most persons contributed no state or federal funds for land acquisition. In a long-overdue innovation, Louisiana now requires recreationists using its wildlife refuges and management areas to buy a special stamp just as a hunter or angler carries a license; no more freeloaders, which is all to the good. Pg.119

11    Like most women, my wife's solicitous concern for wildlife comes naturally from her inordinate maternal instinct. But because of an urban cultural upbringing, she lacks an understanding of the stark survival realities faced daily by every wild beast. Unfortunately, serious sociological problems arise when overly sentimental persons demonstrate greater empathy for "adorable" wild animals (vastly Disney-fied) than for emotionally repulsive *Homo sapiens*. And there then are those who are fanatically pro-choice while at the same time vehemently against killing wild animals —the ultimate incongruity! Pg.119

12    Worse yet, demographers predict that within a comparatively short time, perhaps as early as 2050, our planet's humanity will double to approximately 10 billion souls. This on a finite landmass whose limited resources have already been grievously abused, as witnessed by the multitudes of half-starved, disease-ridden children in the poorest-of-the-poor Third World countries (where 13.5 million children under age 5 die each year from chronic privation). In Africa alone, half of the population is under 20 years in age; the Dark Continent will surely be swamped by the population *tsunami* these baby-boomers are expected to create. Few seem to care much about "primitive" people condemned to a life of squalor and despair, being caught up in more pressing issues, like save the tiger, save the whales, save the escargots. Pg.119

13    In an exhibit featuring firearms owned by Theodore Roosevelt, in his National Park, the caption asked the rhetorical question: "How can a

hunter be a conservationist?" — as if the two activities were mutually exclusive. In answering, the Park Service (by statute a protectionist agency) implied that TR hunted solely to procure specimens for scientific study, which is simply wrong. Roosevelt became interested in taxonomy while still a boy, and therefore realized that museums dearly welcomed donations of zoological specimens, especially collections of exotic mammals from distant lands. Yet no one reading any of his numerous (8) books about hunting can help but conclude that Teddy did not repent killing an animal per se, but instead looked forward to the sporting chase as a "bully" adventure as well as healthful recreation. So much for revisionist history.

Premier ecologist Aldo Leopold remained an ardent hunter till the day he died. This presented a dilemma, however, according to Robert McCabe, who knew Leopold well: "This hunter image, real as indeed it was, is often denied, attacked or lamented by those who would use his writings to support or justify other less constructive stands on the use of our natural resources." Leopold biographer Curt Meine noted that the book *Round River* did not achieve its expected success because the "unrelenting procession of [Leopold's] hunting tales did not sit well with nonhunting conservationists." More explicitly, his love of hunting tarnished the halo of this quasi-deity, in their eyes.

The latter fraternity commonly use the generic term "hunters" in placing blame for the sad plight of certain animals world-wide. It is ludicrous, of course, to lump ethical, licensed sportsmen with the likes of poachers or mercenary/subsistence hunters. To me this represents a clever ploy by which to discredit legitimate sport hunting in hopes of having it banned. One wonders whether these aren't the same persons who take much irreplaceable habitat out of wildlife production in lavishly pursuing the great American dream of *la dolce vita*, the "good life."

Pg.119

# ACKNOWLEDGMENTS

Many persons aided in preparation of this book without knowing it; regrettably, some must remain anonymous because I forgot to jot down their names. I am indebted for various favors to Faye Swanberg (Alger County historian), Robert Lowney (Durand Union Station), James Islieb (Michigan State University Extension Service), Kenneth LaFayette (*Flaming Brands*), John Franzen (U.S. Forest Service), Kathleen Deagan (Florida Museum Natural History), David Armour (Mackinac State Historic Parks), Charles Cleland (Michigan State University Museum), Richard Leep (Michigan State University Extension Service), Scott Jones and Milan Novak (Ontario Ministry Natural Resources), Thomas Friggens (Michigan Iron Industry Museum), LeRoy Barnett (Michigan State Archives), Stanley Jacek (Army Corps of Engineers, "Soo" Locks), James Ecker (Mackinac Bridge Authority), Michael Marsden (Northern Michigan University), Earl Rowley (local trapper), and Robert Wood, Edward Langenau, Clyde Allison, David Kenyon, William Botti, and Leo Perry (all Michigan DNR).

The Peter White Public Library, Northern Michigan University Library, Munising School-Public Library, and National Museum of American Art were helpful in providing valuable references. Rollin Baker's *Michigan Mammals* was a goldmine of life history statistics, as well as being inspirational.

I especially thank long-time colleagues Tony Peterle (Ohio State University), Forest Stearns (University Wisconsin-Milwaukee), Walter Loope (National Park Service), Kenneth Lowe (Michigan Out-of-Doors) and Robert Doepker (Michigan DNR) for helpful reviews of the manuscript. Lastly I proudly acknowledge the abiding interest and filial devotion of son Tom for typing the first draft, and daughter Ann for handling endless revisions of the ms. They both labored mightily to decipher my often illegible script. My long-suffering wife cheerfully put up with me brooding almost incommunicado during the many months holed up in my basement lair writing the text. Through it all we somehow stayed best friends!

# BIBLIOGRAPHY

Ahlgren, C. E., and I. F. Ahlgren. 1983. The human impact on northern forest ecosystems. Pages 33-51 *in* S. L. Flader, ed. The Great Lakes forest. Univ. Minnesota Press, Minneapolis.

Alcoze, T. M. 1981. Pre-settlement beaver density in the Upper Great Lakes region. Ph.D. Dissertation, Michigan State Univ., E. Lansing. 107 pp.

Allen, D. L. 1979. Wolves of Minong. Houghton Mifflin Co., Boston. 499 pp.

Anderson, R. C. 1972. The ecological relationships of meningeal worm and native cervids in North America. J. Wildl. Diseases. 8:304 310.

Anderson, R. C., and A. K. Prestwood. 1981. Lungworms. Pages 266-317 *in* W. R. Davidson, F. A. Hayes, V. F. Nettles, and F. E. Kellogg, eds. Diseases and parasites of white-tailed deer. 2nd Int. white-tailed deer disease symp., Tall Timbers Res. Sta. Misc. Publ. 7.

Anderson, S. J. [1982]. Wildlife habitat changes following 1976 wildfire on the Seney National Wildlife Refuge. U.S. Fish and Wildlife Service. 6 pp.

Armour, D. A., and K. R. Widder. 1980. Michilimackinac: a handbook to the site. Mackinac State Historic Parks, Mackinac Island, Mich. 48 pp.

Arnold, D. A., and R. D. Schofield. 1956. Status of Michigan timber wolves. Michigan Dept. Conserv., Game Div. Rept. 2097. Lansing. 2 pp.

Bailey, V. 1926. Biological survey of North Dakota. North Amer. Fauna. 49:226 pp.

Baker, R. H. 1983. Michigan mammals. Michigan State Univ. Press, E. Lansing. 642 pp.

Begley, S. 1991. A question of breeding. National Wildlife. 29 (2):12-16.

Bergerud, A. T. 1985. Antipredator strategies of caribou: dispersion along shorelines. Can. J. Zool. 63:1324-1329.

Bergerud, A. T., and W. E. Mercer. 1989. Caribou introductions in eastern North America. Wildl. Soc. Bull. 17:111-120.

Bersing, O. S. 1966. A century of Wisconsin deer. Wisconsin Dept. Conserv., Madison. 272 pp.

Bradt, G. W. 1947. Michigan beaver management. Michigan Dept. Conserv., Game Div., Lansing. 56 pp.

Bourdo, E. A. Jr. 1983. The forest the settlers saw. Pages 3-16 *in* S. L.Flader, ed. The Great Lakes forest. Univ. Minnesota Press, Minneapolis.

Burt, W. H. 1948. The mammals of Michigan. Univ. Michigan Press, Ann Arbor. 288 pp.

Carter, J. L. 1986. Introduction. Pages 1-8 *in* C. A. Symon, ed. Alger County: a centennial history, 1885-1985. Bayshore Press, Munising, Mich.

Castle, B. H. 1987. The Grand Island story. Book Concern Printers, Houghton, Mich. 110 pp.

Champlain, S. de. 1922-1936. The works of Samuel de Champlain. H. P. Bigger, ed. 6 vols. The Champlain Society, Toronto.

Cleland, C. E. 1966. The prehistoric animal ecology and ethnozoology of the Upper Great Lakes region. Anthro. Papers 29, Univ. Michigan Museum Anthro., Ann Arbor. 294 pp.

Cleland, C. E. 1982. The inland shore fishery of the northern Great Lakes: its development and importance in prehistory. American Antiquity. 47:761-784.

Cleland, C. E. 1983. Indians in a changing environment. Pages 83-95 *in* S. L. Flader, ed. The Great Lakes forest. Univ. Minnesota Press, Minneapolis.

Cranston, J. H. 1949. Etienne Brule: immortal scoundrel. The Ryerson Press, Toronto. 144 pp.

Cringan, A. T. 1957. History, food habits and range requirements of the woodland caribou of continental North America. Trans. North Amer. Wildl. Conf. 22:485-500.

# BIBLIOGRAPHY

Curtis, J. T. 1959. The vegetation of Wisconsin. Univ. Wisconsin Press, Madison. 672 pp.

Dahlberg, B. L., and R. C. Guettinger. 1956. The white-tailed deer in Wisconsin. Tech. Bull. 14, Wisconsin Dept. Conserv., Madison. 282 pp.

Day, G. M. 1953. The Indian as an ecological factor in the northeastern forests. Ecology. 34: 329-346.

Deagan, K. A. 1992. La Isabela: Europe's first foothold in the New World. National Geographic. 181(1):41-53.

DeLignery, C. N. 1868. Renewal of the Fox War. Wisconsin Hist. Coll. 5:86-91.

Dorr, J. A., Jr., and D. F. Eschman. 1970. Geology of Michigan. Univ. Michigan Press, Ann Arbor. 476 pp.

Earle, R. D. 1978. The fisher-porcupine relationship in Upper Michigan. M.S. Thesis, Michigan Technological Univ., Houghton. 126 pp.

Erickson, A. W., J. Nellor, and G. A. Petrides. 1964. The black bear in Michigan. Agric. Exp. Sta. Res. Bull. 4, Michigan State Univ., E. Lansing. 102 pp.

Fenna, D., O. Schaefer, L. Mix, and J. A. Gilbert. 1971. Ethanol metabolism in various social groups. Can. Med. Assoc. J. 105:472-475.

Franzmann, A. W., C. C. Swartz, and R. O. Peterson. 1980. Moose calf mortality in summer on the Kenai Peninsula, Alaska. J. Wildl. Manage. 44:764-768.

Fritts, S. H., and W. J. Paul. 1989. Interactions of wolves and dogs in Minnesota. Wildl. Soc. Bull. 17:121-123.

Fuller, T. K. 1989. Population dynamics of wolves in north-central Minnesota. Wildl. Monogr. 105. 41 pp.

Fuller, T. K., W. E. Berg, G. L. Radde, M. S. Lenarz, and G. B. Joselyn. 1992. A history and current estimate of wolf distribution and number in Minnesota. Wildl. Soc. Bull. 20:42-55.

Gates, D. M., C. H. D. Clarke, and J. T. Harris. 1983. Wildlife in a changing environment. Pages 52-80 in S. L. Flader, ed. The Great Lakes forest. Univ. Minnesota Press, Minneapolis.

Gibbons, B. 1992. Alcohol, the legal drug. National Geographic. 181(2):2-35.

Gringhuis, D. 1974. Moccasin tracks: a saga of the Michigan Indian. Ed.Bull No.1, Michigan State Univ. Mus., E. Lansing. 32 pp.

Gullion, G. 1989. The ruffed grouse. North Word Press., Minocqua, Wisc. 136 pp.

Harger, E. M. 1965. The status of the Canada lynx in Michigan. Jack-Pine Warbler. 43:150-153.

Harger, E. M., and D. F. Switzenberg. 1958. Returning the pine marten to Michigan. Michigan Dept. Conserv., Game Div. Rept. 2199. Lansing. 7 pp.

Harrington, F.H., and P.C. Paquet, eds. 1982. Wolves of the world: perspectives of behavior, ecology, and conservation. Noyes Publication, Park Ridge, N.J. 474 pp.

Harris, W. J. 1976. The Chequamegon country, 1659-1976. Harris Books, Fayetteville, Ark. 516 pp.

Hash, H. S. 1987. Wolverine. Pages 575-585 in M. Novak, J. A. Baker, M. E. Obbard, B. Mullock, eds. Wild furbearer management and conservation in North America. Ontario Ministry Nat. Res., Toronto.

Hatcher, H. 1950. A century of iron and men. Bobbs-Merrill Co., New York. 295 pp.

Heinselman, M. L. 1973. Fire in the virgin forests of the Boundary Waters Canoe Area, Minnesota. J. Quarternary Res. 3:329-82.

Hendrickson, J., W. L. Robinson, and L. D. Mech. 1975. Status of the wolf in Michigan, 1973. Am. Midl. Nat. 94:226-232.

Hickerson, H. 1965. The Virginia deer and intertribal buffer zones in the Upper Mississippi Valley. Pages 43-65 in A. Leeds and A. Voyda,eds. Man, culture and animals: the role of animals in human ecological adjustments. Amer. Assoc. Advance. Sci., Washington, D. C.

Hickie, P. F. [1943]. Michigan moose. Michigan Dept. Conserv., Game Div., Lansing. 57 pp.

Hope, J. 1994. Wolves and wolf hybrids as pets are big business but a bad idea. Smithsonian. 25(3):34-45.

Hornocker, M. G. 1970. An analysis of mountain lion predation upon mule deer and elk in the Idaho Primitive Area. Wildl. Monogr. 21. 39 pp.

Hornocker, M.G. 1992. Learning to live with mountain lions. National Geographic. 182(1):52-65.

Hornocker, M. G., and H. S. Hash. 1981. Ecology of the wolverine in northwestern Montana. Can. J. Zool. 59:1286-1301.

Idso, S. B. 1990. The carbon dioxide/trace gas greenhouse effect. Pages 19-26 in B. A. Kimbell, ed. Impact of carbon dioxide, trace gases and climate change on global agriculture. Amer. Soc. Agronomy Spec. Publ.53.

Irvine, G. W., L. T. Magnus, and B. J. Bradle. 1964. The restocking of fisher in Lake States forests. Trans. North Amer. Wildl. Conf. 29:307-314.

Jackson, H. H. T. 1961. Mammals of Wisconsin. Univ. Wisconsin Press, Madison. 504 pp.

Jenkins, D. H. 1949. A report on the otter in Michigan. Michigan Dept. Conserv., Game Div. Rept. 1037. Lansing. 7 pp.

Johnson, D. R. 1969. Returns of the American Fur Company, 1835-1839. J. Mammal. 50:836-839.

Johnson, I. A. 1919. The Michigan fur trade. Michigan Historical Comm. Univ. Serv., Lansing. 201 pp.

Karamanski, T. J. 1989. Deep woods frontier: a history of logging in northern Michigan. Wayne State Univ. Press, Detroit. 305 pp.

Kay, J. 1979. Wisconsin hunting patterns, 1634-1836. Annals Assoc. Amer. Geographers. 69:402-418.

Kellum F. 1941. Cusino's captive moose. Michigan Conservation. 10(7):4-5.

Kuenzer, D. 1986. The Tannery. Pages 202-205, in C. A. Symon, ed. Alger County: a centennial history, 1885-1985. Bayshore Press, Munising, Mich.

LaFayette, K.D. 1990. Flaming brands. Northern Michigan Univ. Press, Marquette. 112 pp.

Landes, R. 1938. The Ojibwa woman. Columbia Univ. Press, New York. 247 pp

Lankton, L. 1991. Cradle to grave: life, work, and death at the Lake Superior copper mines. Oxford Univ. Press, New York, Oxford. 319 pp.

Lawrence, W. H., L. D. Fay, and S. A. Graham. 1956. A report on the beaver die-off in Michigan. J. Wildl. Manage. 20:184-187.

Laycock, W. E. 1960. No place for reindeer! Michigan Conservation. 39(2):12-16.

Leopold, A. 1933. Game management. Charles Schribner's Sons., New York. 481 pp.

Leopold, A. 1949. A Sand County almanac. Oxford Univ. Press, New York. 226 pp.

Longfellow, H. W. 1863. The complete poetical works of Longfellow. Houghton Mifflin Co., Boston, New York. 655 pp.

Loope, W. L. 1991. Interrelationship of fire history, land use history, and landscape pattern within Pictured Rocks National Lakeshore. Can. Field-Nat. 105:18-28.

Loucks, O. L. 1983. New lights on the changing forest. Pages 17-32 in S.L. Flader, ed. The Great Lakes forest. Univ. Minnesota Press, Minneapolis.

Manville, R. H. 1948. The vertebrate fauna of the Huron Mountains, Michigan. Am. Midl. Nat. 39:615-640.

Manville, R. H. 1950. The wolverine in Michigan. Jack-Pine Warbler. 28:127-129.

Martin, C. 1978. Keepers of the game: Indian-animal relationships and the fur trade. Univ. California Press, Berkeley. 453 pp.

Matthews, S. W. 1990. Under the sun — is our world warming? National Geographic. 178(4):66-99.

McCabe, R.A. 1987. Aldo Leopold/the professor. Rusty Rock Press, Madison, Wisc. 172 pp.

McCabe, R. E., and T. R. McCabe. 1984. Of slings and arrows: an historical retrospection. Pages 19-72 in L. K. Halls, ed. White-tailed deer: ecology and management. Stackpole Books, Harrisburg, Penn.

McCullough, D. R. 1979. The George Reserve deer herd: population ecology of a K-selected species. Univ. Michigan Press, Ann Arbor. 271 pp.

Mech, L. D. 1977. Wolf pack buffer zones as prey reservoirs. Science. 198:320-321.

Mech, L. D. 1984. Predators and predation. Pages 189-200 in L. K. Halls, ed. White-tailed deer: ecology and management. Stackpole Books, Harrisburg, Penn.

# BIBLIOGRAPHY

Meine, C. 1988. Aldo Leopold: his life and work. Univ. Wisconsin Press, Madison. 638 pp.

Melillo, J.M., and J.E. Hobbie. 1986. Ecosystem alteration of boreal forest streams by beaver *(Castor canadensis)*. Ecology. 67:1254-1269.

Messick, J. P., and M. G. Hornocker. 1981. Ecology of the badger in southwestern Idaho. Wildl. Monogr. 76. 53 pp.

Moran, R. J. 1973. The Rocky Mountain elk in Michigan. Michigan. Dept. Nat. Res., Wildl. Div. Rept. 267. Lansing. 93 pp.

Murdock, W. A. 1943. Boom copper. Book Concern Printers, Hancock, Mich. 255 pp.

National Park Service. 1990. Grand Portage National Monument, Minnesota. National Park Service brochure.

Osborn, C. S., and S. Osborn. 1944. "Hiawatha", with its original Indian legends. The Jacques Cattell Press, Lancaster, Penn. 255 pp.

Ozoga, J. J., and L. J. Verme. 1966. Noteworthy locality records for some Upper Michigan mammals. Jack-Pine Warbler. 44:52.

Ozoga, J. J., and L. J. Verme. 1982. Predation by black bear on new-born white-tailed deer. J. Mammal. 63: 695-696.

Ozoga, J. J., and L. J. Verme. 1986. Relation of maternal age to fawn rearing success in white-tailed deer. J. Wildl. Manage. 50:480-486.

Payne, S. J., 1982. Fire in America: a cultural history of wildland and rural fire. Princeton Univ. Press, Princeton, N.J. 654 pp.

Peek, J. M., *et al.* 1991. Restoration of wolves in North America. The Wildlife Soc. Tech. Rev. 91-1. 21pp.

Peterle, T. J. 1954. An observation on otter feeding. J. Wildl. Manage. 18:141-142.

Peterle, T. J. 1975. Deer sociobiology. Wildl. Soc. Bull. 3:82-83.

Peterson, R. O. 1977. Wolf ecology and prey relationships on Isle Royale. National Park Service Sci. Monogr. Series no. 11. 210 pp.

Peterson, R. O. 1989. Ecological studies of wolves on Isle Royale. Annual Report Isle Royale Nat. History Assoc., Houghton, Mich. 14 pp.

Peterson, E. T. 1979. Hunter's heritage: a history of hunting in Michigan. Michigan United Conserv. Clubs, Lansing. 54 pp.

Powell, R. A., and R. Earle. 1981. Fisher and porcupine: an odd couple. Michigan Out-of-Doors. 35 (12):42-45.

Presnall, C. C. 1943. Wildlife conservation as affected by American Indian and Caucasian concepts. J. Mammal. 24:458-464.

Quick, H.F. 1953. Wolverine, fisher, and marten studies in a wilderness region. Trans. North Amer. Wildl. Conf. 18:513-532.

Radisson, P. E. 1882. Fourth voyage. Wisconsin Hist. Coll. 11:71-96.

Ray, A. J. 1987. The fur trade in North America: an overview from a historical geographic perspective. Pages 21-30 *in* M. Novak, J. A. Baker, M. E. Obbard, and B. Mullock, eds. Wild furbearer management and conservation in North America. Ontario Ministry Nat. Res., Toronto.

Reed, T. E., H. Kalant, R. J. Griffins, B. M. Kapur, and J. G. Rankin. 1976. Alcohol and acetaldehydemetabolism in Caucasian, Chinese, and Americans. Can. Med. Assoc. J. 115:851-855.

Rex, D. K., W. F. Bosion, J. E. Smialek, and T. K. Li. 1985. Alcohol and aldehyde dehydrogenase isoenzymes in North American Indians. Alcoholism Clinic. and Exp. Res. 9:147-152.

Robinson, W.L., and G.J. Smith. 1977. Observations on recently killed wolves in Upper Michigan. Wildl. Soc. Bull. 5:25-26.

Rogers, L. L. 1987. Effects of food supply and kinship on social behavior, movements, and population growth of black bears in northeastern Minnesota. Wildl. Monogr. 97. 72 pp.

Rogers, L.L., D.W. Kuehn, A.W. Erickson, E.M. Harger, L.J. Verme, and J.J. Ozoga. 1976. Characteristics and management of black bears feeding in garbage dumps, campgrounds, or residential areas. Pages 169-175 *in* Bears — their biology and management. IUCN. Morges, Switzerland.

Samuel, W. M., M. J. Pybus, D. A. Welch, and C. J. Wilke. 1992. Elk as a potential host for meningeal worm: implications for translocation. J. Wildl. Manage. 54:629-639.

Schaeffer, J. A., and W. O. Pruitt, Jr. 1991. Fire and woodland caribou in southeastern Manitoba. Wildl. Monogr. 116. 39 pp.

Schoolcraft, H. R. 1851. Personal memoirs of a residency of fifty years with Indian tribes on the American frontier: with brief notices of passing events, facts, and opinions, A.D. 1812 to A.D. 1842. Lippencott, Grambo & Co., Philadelphia. 703 pp.

Schoolcraft. H. L. 1856. The myth of Hiawatha and other oral legends. J.B. Lippincott & Co. Philadelphia. Reprinted in 1984 by Avery Studios, AuTrain, Mich. 272 pp.

Schroger, A. W. 1940. Wolverine in Michigan. J. Mammal. 20:503.

Schroger, A. W. 1948. Further records of the wolverine for Wisconsin and Michigan. J. Mammal. 29:295.

Shiras, G. III. 1936. Hunting wild life with camera and flashlight. Vol. 1, National Geographic Soc., Washington, D.C. 450 pp.

Silver, H. 1968. History. Pages 15-28 *in* H.R. Siegler, ed. The white-tailed deer of New Hampshire. Survey Rep. 10. N.H. Fish Game Dept., Concord.

Stearns, F. 1951. The composition of the sugar maple-hemlock-yellow birch association in northern Wisconsin. Ecology. 32:243-265.

Stearns, F. 1987. The changing forest of the Lakes States. Pages 25-35 *in* W. E. Shands, ed. The Lake States forests — a resources renaissance. Proc. Governors' Conf. Forestry, Minneapolis.

Stearns, F. 1990. Forest history and management in the northern Midwest. Pages 107-122 *in* J.M. Sweeney, ed. Management of dynamic ecosystems. North Cent. Section Wildl. Soc., West Lafayette, Ind.

Stebler, A. M. 1944. The status of the wolf in Michigan. J. Mammal. 25:37-43.

Stebler, A. M. 1951. The ecology of Michigan coyotes and wolves. Ph.D Dissertation, Univ. Michigan, Ann Arbor. 198 pp.

Stephenson, R. 1991. Under the microscope. Alaska. 57(5):28-29.

Swanberg, F. 1986. Munising Township. Pages 13-40 *in* C. A. Symon, ed. Alger County: a centennial history, 1885-1985. Bayshore Press, Munising, Mich.

Swanberg, F. 1986. AuTrain Township. Pages 69-95 *in* C. A. Symon, ed. Alger County: a centennial history, 1885-1985. Bayshore Press, Munising, Mich.

Swanberg, F. 1986. Cleveland - Cliffs Iron Company. Pages 184-190 *in* C. A Symon, ed. Alger County: a centennial history, 1885-1985. Bayshore Press, Munising, Mich.

Swift, E. 1946. A history of Wisconsin deer. Publ. 323, Wisconsin Dept. Conserv., Madison. 96 pp.

Tanner, H. H. 1987. Atlas of Great Lakes Indian history. Univ. Oklahoma Press, Norman. 224 pp.

Terrell, J. V., and D. M. Terrell. 1974. Indian women of the western morning. The Dial Press, New York. 214 pp.

Thiel, R. P. 1985. Relationship between road densities and wolf habitat suitability in Wisconsin. Am. Midl. Nat. 113:404-407.

Thiel, R. P. 1993. The timber wolf in Wisconsin. Univ. Wisconsin Press, Madison. 253 pp.

Thurber, J. M., R. O. Peterson, T. D. Drummer, and S. A. Thomasma. 1994. Gray wolf response to refuge boundaries and roads in Alaska. Wild. Soc. Bull. 22:61-68.

Thwaites, R. G., ed. 1896-1901. The Jesuit relations and allied documents: travels and explorations of the Jesuit missionaries in New France, 1610-1791. 73 volumes. Burrows Brothers, Cleveland.

Tubbs, C. H., and L. J. Verme. 1972. How to create wildlife openings in northern hardwoods. U.S. Forest Service, North Cent. For. Exp. Sta., St. Paul, Minn. 5 pp.

Van Dyke, F. G., and R. H. Brocke. 1987. Sighting and track reports as indices of mountain lion presence. Wildl. Soc. Bull. 15:251-256.

Veatch, J. O. 1953. Soils and land of Michigan. Michigan State College Press, E. Lansing. 241 pp.

Veatch, J. O. 1959. Map of presettlement forest in Upper Michigan. Michigan State Univ., Dept. Resource Development, E. Lansing.

Veatch, J. O., L. P. Schoenmann, F. R. Lesh, and Z. C. Foster. 1929. Soil survey of Alger County, Michigan. U.S. Dept Agri. Bull. 32. 41 pp.

Verano, J. W., and O. H. Ubelaker. 1991. Health and disease in the pre-Columbian world. Pages 208-223 *in* H. J. Viola and C. Margolis, eds. Seeds of changes: five hundred years since Columbus. Smithsonian Institution Press, Washington, London.

Verme, L. J. 1961. Production of white-cedar browse by logging. J. Forestry. 58:589-591.

Verme, L. J. 1965. Swamp conifer deeryards in northern Michigan: their ecology and management. J. Forestry. 63:523-529.

Verme, L. J. 1968. An index of winter weather severity for northern deer. J. Wildl. Manage. 32:566-574.

Verme, L. J. 1970. Some characteristics of captive Michigan moose. J.Mammal. 51:403-405.

Verme, L. J. 1973. Movements of white-tailed deer in Upper Michigan. J. Wildl. Manage. 37:543-552.

Verme, L. J. 1977. Assessment of natal mortality in Upper Michigan deer. J. Wildl. Manage. 41:700-708.

Verme, L. J. 1983. Sex ratio variation in Odocoileus: a critical review. J. Wildl. Manage. 46:573-582.

Verme, L. J. 1984. Some background on moose in Upper Michigan. Michigan Dept. Nat. Res., Wildl. Div. Rept. 2973. Lansing. 6 pp.

Verme, L. J. 1988. Lipogenesis in buck fawn white-tailed deer: photoperiod effects. J. Mammal. 69:67-70.

Verme, L. J. 1991. Decline in doe fawn fertility in southern Michigan deer. Can. J. Zool. 69:25-28.

Verme, L. J., and W. F. Johnston. 1986. Regeneration of northern white cedar deeryards in Upper Michigan. J. Wildl. Manage. 50:307-313.

Verme, L. J., and J. J. Ozoga. 1980. Effects of diet on growth and lipogenesis in deer fawns. J. Wildl. Manage. 44:315-324.

Verme, L. J., and D. E. Ullrey. 1984. Physiology and nutrition. Pages 91-118 in L. K. Halls, ed. White-tailed deer: ecology and management. Stackpole Books, Harrisburg, Penn.

Vogel, R. J. 1970. Fire and the northern Wisconsin pine barrens. Proc. fire ecology conf., Tall Timbers Res. Sta. 10:175-209.

Waters, T. F. 1987. The Superior North Shore. Univ. Minnesota Press, Minneapolis. 361 pp.

Wilkinson, A. 1990. The uncommitted crime. Pages 61-118 in The New Yorker (November 20).

Wood, N. A., and L. R. Dice. 1924. Records of the distribution of Michigan mammals. Michigan Acad. Sci., Arts, Letters. 3:425-469

Worth, J. 1979. A series of three articles on logging of white cedar in the U. P., in the Upper Peninsula Sunday Times, Escanaba, Mich.

# SCIENTIFIC NAMES

## PLANTS

| | |
|---|---|
| Balsam fir | *Abies balsamea* |
| Balsam poplar | *Populus balsamifera* |
| Basswood | *Tilia americana* |
| Bean | *Phaseolus* |
| Beech | *Fagus grandifolia* |
| Bigtooth aspen | *Populus grandidentata* |
| Black spruce | *Picea mariana* |
| Blueberry | *Vaccinium* |
| Corn | *Zea mays* |
| Cottonwood | *Populus deltoides* |
| Elm | *Ulmus* |
| Fireweed | *Epilobium angustifolium* |
| Hemlock | *Tsuga canadensis* |
| Hickory | *Carya* |
| Jack pine | *Pinus banksiana* |
| Morel | *Morchella* |
| Oak | *Quercus* |
| Old-man's-beard | *Usnea* |
| Paper birch | *Betula papyrifera* |
| Raspberry | *Rubus* |
| Red pine | *Pinus resinosa* |
| Reindeer lichen | *Cladonia* |
| Sedge | *Carex* |
| Squash | *Curcubita* |
| Sugar maple | *Acer saccharum* |
| Tamarack | *Larix laricina* |
| Trembling aspen | *Populus tremuloides* |
| White cedar | *Thuja occidentalis* |
| White pine | *Pinus strobus* |
| White spruce | *Picea glauca* |
| Wild rice | *Zizania aquatica* |
| Yellow birch | *Betula alleghaniensis* |

## ANIMALS

| | |
|---|---|
| Badger | *Taxidea taxus* |
| Beaver | *Castor canadensis* |
| Bison | *Bison bison* |
| Black bear | *Ursus americanus* |
| Blackfly | *Simulium* |
| Black-footed ferret | *Mustela nigripes* |
| Bobcat | *Felis rufus* |
| Canada goose | *Branta canadensis* |
| Coyote | *Canis latrans* |
| Elephant seal | *Mirounga angustirostris* |
| Elk | *Cervus elaphus* |
| Ermine | *Mustela erminea* |
| Fallow deer | *Dama dama* |
| Fisher | *Martes pennanti* |
| Gray fox | *Urocyon cinereoargenteus* |
| Gray wolf | *Canis lupus* |
| Great blue heron | *Andrea herodias* |
| Kirtland's warbler | *Dendroica kirtlandii* |
| Lake trout | *Salvelinus namaycush* |
| Lynx | *Felis lynx* |
| Marten | *Martes americana* |

# SCIENTIFIC NAMES

Masked shrew . . . . . . . . . . . . *Sorex cinereus*
Mastodon . . . . . . . . . . . . . . . *Mammut americanus*
Mink . . . . . . . . . . . . . . . . . *Mustela vison*
Moose . . . . . . . . . . . . . . . . . *Alces alces*
Mosquito . . . . . . . . . . . . . . *Culex*
Mountain lion . . . . . . . . . . *Felis concolor*
Muskrat . . . . . . . . . . . . . . . . *Ondatra zibethicus*
Nene . . . . . . . . . . . . . . . . . . *Branta sandvicensis*
Northern pike . . . . . . . . . . . . *Esox lucius*
Otter . . . . . . . . . . . . . . . . . . *Lutra canadensis*
Porcupine . . . . . . . . . . . . . *Erethizon dorsatum*
Prairie chicken . . . . . . . . . . . *Tympanuchus cupido*
Raccoon . . . . . . . . . . . . . . . . *Procyon lotor*
Red fox . . . . . . . . . . . . . . . *Vulpes vulpes*
Red squirrel . . . . . . . . . . . . . *Tamiasciurus hudsonicus*
Red wolf . . . . . . . . . . . . . . . . *Canis niger*
Reindeer . . . . . . . . . . . . . . . *Rangifer tarandus*

Roe deer . . . . . . . . . . . . . . . . *Capreolus capreolus*
Ruffed grouse . . . . . . . . . . . . *Bonasa umbellus*
Sandhill crane . . . . . . . . . . . *Grus canadensis*
Sharp-tailed grouse . . . . . . . *Pedioecetes phasianellus*
Snapping turtle . . . . . . . . . . *Chelydra serpentina*
Snowshoe hare . . . . . . . . . . . *Lepus americanus*
Sturgeon . . . . . . . . . . . . . . . *Acipenser fulvescens*
Thirteen-lined ground squirrel . *Spermophilus tridecemlineatus*
Trumpeter swan . . . . . . . . . . *Cygnus buccinator*
Whitefish . . . . . . . . . . . . . . . *Coregonus clupeaformis*
White-tailed deer . . . . . . . . . . *Odocoileus virginianus*
Whooping crane . . . . . . . . . . *Grus americana*
Wolverine . . . . . . . . . . . . . . . *Gulo gulo*
Woodchuck . . . . . . . . . . . . . *Marmota monax*
Woodcock . . . . . . . . . . . . . . *Philohela minor*
Woodland caribou . . . . . . . . . *Rangifer tarandus*

# UPPER MICHIGAN MAMMALS[1]

Virginia oppossum . . . . . . . . *Didelphis virginiana*
Arctic shrew . . . . . . . . . . . . . *Sorex arcticus*
Smokey shrew . . . . . . . . . . . . *Sorex fumeus*
Pygmy shrew . . . . . . . . . . . . . *Sorex hoyi*
Water shrew . . . . . . . . . . . . . *Sorex palustris*
Short-tailed shrew . . . . . . . . *Blarina brevicauda*
Star-nosed mole . . . . . . . . . . *Condylura cristata*
Keen's bat . . . . . . . . . . . . . . *Myotis keenii*
Little brown bat . . . . . . . . . . *Myotis lucifugus*
Silver-haired bat . . . . . . . . . *Lasionycteris noctivagans*
Eastern pipistrelle . . . . . . . . *Pipistrellus subflavus*
Big brown bat . . . . . . . . . . . *Eptesicus fuscus*
Red bat . . . . . . . . . . . . . . . . *Lasiurus borealis*
Hoary bat . . . . . . . . . . . . . . *Lasiurus cinereus*
Eastern cottontail . . . . . . . . . *Sylvilagus floridanus*
European hare . . . . . . . . . . . *Lepus capensis*
Eastern chipmunk . . . . . . . . *Tamias striatus*
Least chipmunk . . . . . . . . . . *Eutamias minimus*

Gray squirrel . . . . . . . . . . . . . *Sciurus carolinensis*
Fox squirrel . . . . . . . . . . . . . *Scuirus niger*
Northern flying squirrel . . . . *Glaucomys sabrinus*
Southern flying squirrel . . . . *Glaucomys volans*
White-footed mouse . . . . . . . *Peromyscus leucopus*
Deer mouse . . . . . . . . . . . . . *Peromyscus maniculatus*
Southern red-backed mole . . . *Clethrionomys gapperi*
Meadow vole . . . . . . . . . . . . *Microtus pennsylvanicus*
Southern bog lemming . . . . . *Synaptomys cooperi*
Norway rat . . . . . . . . . . . . . . *Rattus norvegicus*
House mouse . . . . . . . . . . . . *Mus musculus*
Meadow jumping mouse . . . . *Zapus hudsonius*
Woodland jumping mouse . . . . *Napaeozapus insignis*
Long-tailed weasel . . . . . . . . *Mustela frenata*
Least weasel . . . . . . . . . . . . . *Mustela nivalis*
Striped skunk . . . . . . . . . . . *Mephitis mephitis*

[1] According to R. H. Baker, 1983, Michigan Mammals. Other than those listed in text.

# GLOSSARY

**Asbestos forest:** Said of northern hardwood forests because the humid, fuel-free understory makes them virtually immune to fire.

**Anthropomorphism:** Attributing a human-like characteristic to a lower animal.

**Balance of nature:** The hypothetical state of equilibrium between animal species or an animal and its environment

**Bioenergetic:** The realm or physical laws of energy and its transformation in an organism.

**Canids:** Any member of the dog family, or Canidae.

**Carrying capacity:** The innate ability of a parcel of land to support a given population of (game) animals in good health over time.

**Catabolism:** The biological process by which living tissue is destroyed or changed into waste products by the body, as during starvation.

**Cervid:** Any member of the deer family (Cervidae) in which the male grows renewable antlers of solid bone annually, in contrast to permanent horns.

**Clearcut:** The harvesting of trees which removes all (silvicultural) or almost all (commercial) mature stems in a stand.

**Climax:** An ecological concept applied to the final, self-perpetuating community of plants that develop under a particular climate or soil, as long as these conditions prevail.

**Clonal:** A means of asexual reproduction from a single individual, as by root-suckers in aspen.

**Coppice:** The asexual reproduction of a plant by production of stump sprouts, especially after the tree is cut down.

**Corduroy road:** A trail or path made by placing cut logs side by side, usually for crossing a swampy site.

**Demography:** The science of vital statistics dealing with the distribution and density of a given population.

**Discombobulate:** To upset, or disconcert, the normal composure or behavior of an animal.

**Estrus:** The period when a female will accept a male for mating because of a hormonal compulsion commonly termed heat period, or rut, in cervids.

**Extirpation:** The killing, or extermination, of all members of a species or a group.

**Fecundity:** A quantitative term, meaning the number of young conceived or reared per litter or over a lifetime.

**Fertility:** The qualitative aspect of reproduction, or the ability to produce offspring, beginning at puberty and ending at sexual senescence.

**Forb:** Any of a broad-leaved flowering plant, or an herbaceous species, as distinguished form grasses, sedges, etc.

**Genotype:** An individual within a group, each having the same hereditary, or genetic, attributes.

**Hierarchy:** In animals, the arrangement of individuals within a group from lowest to highest dominance rank.

**High-grade:** In logging work, the harvesting of only the best-quality tree from a stand.

**Igneous:** A rock formation produced from molten magma by the action of fire, as in volcanic activity.

**Inanition:** The lack of strength, or exhaustion, resulting form lack of food or an inability to assimilate it.

**Indigenous:** A native-born person, one belonging to a particular region or country.

**Internecine:** The killing or destruction of individuals on both sides of a kindred group, as in a civil war.

**Lipogenesis:** The production, for body storage, of fats or lipid-like substances; usually a seasonal event under hormonal control.

**Menarche:** The first menstrual period of a woman upon reaching puberty.

**Mustelid:** A member of the weasel family, Mustelidae.

**Omnivore:** A species that can and will eat both plant and animal food.

**Podzol:** The development of soils, especially in cool, humid regions, in which the upper layers are leached of minerals that then concentrate in underlying layers (horizons).

**Population cycle:** The concept of rhythmic fluctuation in animal abundance. The temporal scale of highs and lows occur at 10-year intervals in ruffed grouse and snowshoe hares, for example, and correlates closely with ongoing sun-spot cycles.

**Prescribed fire:** The deliberate burning of an area, under safety constraints, to achieve a particular management goal.

**Primordial:** Existing from the beginning or in earlier time, as in primeval.

**Pristine:** Still in original or untouched state, as in old-growth or virgin timber.

**Radiant energy:** Light , or heat, traveling in electromagnetic waves; it differs markedly from heat flux via conduction or convection.

**Rotation cycle;** In forestry, the age at which trees have reached the most desirable commercial size or quality and are ready to be harvested.

**Ruminant:** Any hoofed, cud-chewing mammal, like a cow or deer, which have a unique stomach with four distinct chambers.

**Scrapes:** The pawing away of litter and soil by a dominant buck, which he urinates on to advertise his presence to does and lesser males. They are located underneath an overhanging limb so that the buck can smear it with attractants (pheromones) from facial glands.

**Sedentary:** Said of an animal that remains in one locality, and does not move around much nor migrates with the seasons.

**Selection logging:** A silvicultural method in which only trees of optimum or mature size are harvested during periodic logging.

**Taiga:** A Russian term meaning a forest of small conifer trees that grow (slowly) in cold, far-northern climes.

**Taxonomy:** The science and practice of arranging plants and animals in natural orders based on common distinguishing physical characteristics.

**Torpidity:** A state in which an animal becomes sluggish or slow in moving, or loses all motion and has minimal bodily functions, as during true hibernation.

**Treponemal disease:** An illness caused by microscopic organisms, such as syphilis and yaws, which is pathogenic to man.

**Tsunami:** A Japanese word meaning a huge wave caused by a violent submarine disturbance or shock, as from an earthquake.

**Tularemia:** An infectious disease of rodents caused by a bacterium which can be transmitted to man in handling infected carcasses.

**Ubiquitous:** Very common or seemingly present everywhere within a wide area.

**Wilderness:** An uninhabited, uncultivated region still in its pristine state.

# A NOTE ON HIAWATHA

"I have at length hit upon a plan for a poem on the American Indians, which seems to me the right one and the only. It is to weave together their beautiful traditions into a whole. I have hit upon a measure, too, which I think the right and only one for such a theme," wrote Henry Wadsworth Longfellow in his diary June 22, 1854.[1] His poem was *The Song of Hiawatha,* published in November of 1855, and which may have been the most immediately popular poem in the English language. "The poem sold 10,000 copies the first four weeks and 30,000 in six months."[2]

*The Song of Hiawatha* was based on Henry Rowe Schoolcraft's (1793 - 1864) studies of Indians in Michigan. Married to the daughter of a Chippewa chief, he gathered much of his Indian lore from his wife. As superintendent of Indian affairs for Michigan (1836 – 1841), he wrote his explorations and researches in a number of highly influential books. The first white man to translate Indian poetry, he was among the first seriously to study Indian legend and religion. Schoolcraft was also a respected scientist, especially in the field of mineralogy. He traveled extensively in the Upper Great Lakes and in 1832 discovered the source of the Mississippi, at Lake Itasca, Minnesota.

The poem is about Hiawatha, an Ojibway Indian, reared by his grandmother, Nokomis, daughter of the Moon. After detailing the hero's accumulation of wisdom, the poet recounts the deeds of Hiawatha in revenging his mother, Wenonah, against his father, the West Wind. Hiawatha eventually becomes the leader of his people, teaching peace with the white man, although Longfellow implies that Hiawatha had grave misgivings concerning the welfare of the Ojibway people with the whites. When his wife, Minnehaha, dies of starvation, he goes with her to the land of the Northwest Wind in his canoe.

Henry Wadsworth Longfellow (1817 - 1882), author of the poem, was an American poet, translator, romancer, and college professor. He attended Bowdoin College, and later taught languages at Harvard. Longfellow also wrote *Evangeline, The Golden Legend, The Courtship of Miles Standish,* and *Tales of a Wayside Inn.* He died in Cambridge, Massachusetts, in 1882. Some critics of *The Song of Hiawatha* including Edgar Allen Poe, accused Longfellow of plagiarizing the poetic measure used in the ancient Finnish epic the *Kalevala.* But Longfellow, an authentic genius, scoffed at this notion. Literary scholars generally have concluded that, although the narrative styles may be similar in some respects, the similarities in plot appear to be purely coincidental.

1. William Sloan Kennedy, *Henry Wadsworth Longfellow.* (Cambridge, Mass., 1882) p. 85.

2. Cecil B. Williams, *Henry Wadsworth Longfellow.* (Twayne Publishers, Inc., New York, 1964) p. 157.

# INDEX

Alcohol, 38, 121

Algonquin
  Provincial Park, 90, 95, 101

Allen, Durward,101

American Fur
  Company, 43, 45, 49, 52

Aspen, 35, 75, 79

Astor, John, 43, 45


Badger, 110-112

Baker, Rollin, 103, 135

Balsam poplar, 59

Bay Furnace
  (see also Onota), 57, 122

Bears, 51, 90-91, 113-116

Beavers, 44, 47, 113-114

Beech, 21-22, 75

Black-Robes, 38-40

Boreal forest, 21, 29

Brain worm, 87-88, 93

Brule, Etienne, 43

Burgess, Thornton, 117

Burt, William, 107


Canadian Shield, 17

Canids, 95-102, 136

Champlain, Samuel, 32-34

Charcoal, 54-58, 121-122

Chippewas, 41, 47

Clearcut, 55, 72, 74-75, 83, 122

Climate, 18-19, 85

Climax forest, 21, 136

Copper, 55, 60

Corn (maize), 28

Courier de bois, 43

Coyote, 101-102

Deer (see white-tailed)

Deeryards, 76-77, 83-84

Disease, 38-39, 121, 137


Elk, 51, 92-93

Erickson, Albert, 116

Estivant Pines, 22


Famine, 36, 52, 85

Farming, 59-60, 72-73

Fayette, 58, 122

Felt hats, 44, 113

Fire,
  natural, 24-25, 68-70
  prescribed burn, 34-35,
  71, 77-78, 137
  slashings, 68-69, 74, 78

Fisher, 91, 108-110

Fort Michilimackinac, 47-49

French River, 43, 46

Fox,
  red, 102
  grey, 102

Fur trade, 43-53


Geology, 16-17

Glaciation, 16-17

Global warming,18, 22, 86,
  122

Grand Island, 21, 52, 71,
  92-93, 100

Grand Portage, 46, 49-50

Greenhouse effect, 18, 22,
  122

Grosseiliers, Sieur, 42-43


Hartwick Pines, 23-24

Hatcher, Harlan, 58, 122

Hemlock, 21, 73, 75

Hiawatha, 27-32, 36, 40,
  139

Hickie, Paul, 51

Hudson's Bay Company, 43

Hunting methods, 27, 29,
  32-34


Ice age,17, 24

Indians, 27-42, 81

Iron ore, 54-57, 122

Iroquois, 41

Isle Royale, 88, 90, 100-101


Jack pine, 24, 121

Jackson, Hartley, 95, 112

James Bay, 43

Jesuits, 38-40, 49, 88

Johnson, Ida, 45, 47


Kingston Plains, 68, 121

Kirtland's warbler, 22, 123


Lafayette, Kenneth, 55

Lake Huron, 18, 46

Lake Michigan, 18, 28, 38, 43

Lake Superior, 18, 21,
  28-29, 38, 42

Late Woodland Indians, 28, 36

Leopold, Aldo, 13, 96, 117, 124

Longfellow, Henry, 28-29,
  36, 139

Lynx, 91, 104-105


Marten, 108-110

Minnesota, 25, 97, 100

Montreal, 46-48, 50

Moose, 28, 51, 88-90

Mountain lion, 52, 91, 103

Northern hardwoods, 20-22, 75

North West Company, 43, 45-46, 49

Ojibway, 28-29, 34-35, 39

Onota
(see also Bay Furnace), 57, 122

Osborn, Chase & Stillanova, 41

Otter, 110-112

Pelts, 43-44

Peshtigo, 68-69

Peterson, Rolf, 100-101

Pictured Rocks, 28, 34

Pigeon River, 46, 49

Pig iron, 54, 122

Porcupine, 109-110, 117

Radisson, Pierre, 42-43, 51-52

Railroads, 64-66, 71

Red pine, 24, 121

Reindeer
(see also woodland caribou)

Ruffed grouse, 118-119

Saint Mary's River, 43, 46, 90

Sault Ste. Marie, 22, 41, 46, 49, 108

Schoolcraft, Henry, 28, 40, 139

Sex ratios, 82-83

Sharp-tailed grouse, 67, 70

Shiras, George, 86-87, 91, 105

Snowshoe hare, 28, 110

Soils, 17, 21-22, 121

"Soo." 55

Stebler, Adolph, 96

Sugar maple, 21-22, 29, 55

Syphilis, 38, 121, 137

Taiga, 21, 137

Tannery, 73

Thirteen-lined
ground squirrel, 112

Traps, 38, 113

Upper Great Lakes, 21, 28, 35, 74

Upper Michigan, 11, 13, 16-25

Voyageurs, 45, 47

White cedar, 24-25, 60-62, 65, 76, 83

Whitefish Bay, 41

White pine, 22-24, 63, 65-68, 121

White-tailed deer, 32-34, 51, 80-88, 90, 95, 123

Wild rice, 28

Winter-kill, 18, 85

Wisconsin, 35, 52, 68, 97-98

Wolf, 91, 95-101, 122

Wolverine, 52, 91, 106-108

Woodchuck, 110

Woodland caribou, 28, 51, 90-92

Worth, Jean, 60-61

# ORDER INFORMATION

## Hiawatha's Brothers: A Wildlife Retrospective

If your local bookstore is unable to obtain this book,
you may order directly from:

**Avanti Publishing**
R.R. 1, Box 598
Munising, MI 49862